"With great sensitivity and warmth, Fran reminds us that in the shakiest times in our lives, we can lean on our unshakable faith in God in order to carry on."

CYNTHIA SPELL HUMBERT, Christian counselor, speaker, author of *Deceived by Shame, Desired by God* (NavPress)

"With gentleness and compassion, Fran Sandin helps women see God's faithfulness beyond pain, disappointment, and perplexing dilemmas. *Touching the Clouds* is about ordinary women who placed their faith in our extraordinary God. Through His word, they found courage and their faith was lifted. Read it—you'll be blessed!"

BRENDA WAGGONER, licensed professional counselor, author of *Fairy Tale Faith: Living in the Meantime When You Expected Happily Ever After* (Tyndale)

"*Touching the Clouds* is an excellent resource for working through the biblical and practical steps of healing and hope while living in the midst of your own challenging life story. Expect to be transformed! Thanks, Fran, for lifting my faith."

LUCINDA SECREST MCDOWELL, M.T.S., speaker, author of *Amazed by Grace* (Quiet Waters Publications)

D1526252

God bless you in your journey of faith.

♡ *Fran*

TOUCHING THE
CLOUDS

Encouraging Stories to Make Your Faith Soar

Fran Caffey Sandin

Fran Caffey Sandin

NAVPRESS ®

Bringing Truth to Life
P.O. Box 35001, Colorado Springs, Colorado 80935

OUR GUARANTEE TO YOU

We believe so strongly in the message of our books that we are making this quality guarantee to you. If for any reason you are disappointed with the content of this book, return the title page to us with your name and address and we will refund to you the list price of the book. To help us serve you better, please briefly describe why you were disappointed. Mail your refund request to: NavPress, P.O. Box 35002, Colorado Springs, CO 80935.

The Navigators is an international Christian organization. Our mission is to reach, disciple, and equip people to know Christ and to make Him known through successive generations. We envision multitudes of diverse people in the United States and every other nation who have a passionate love for Christ, live a lifestyle of sharing Christ's love, and multiply spiritual laborers among those without Christ.

NavPress is the publishing ministry of The Navigators. NavPress publications help believers learn biblical truth and apply what they learn to their lives and ministries. Our mission is to stimulate spiritual formation among our readers.

Cover design by Ray Moore
Cover photo by Randy Schwartz / Brand X Pictures
Creative Team: Nanci McAlister, Greg Clouse, Cara Iverson, Laura Spray, Pat Miller

Some of the anecdotal illustrations in this book are true to life and are included with the permission of the persons involved. All other illustrations are composites of real situations, and any resemblance to people living or dead is coincidental.

Unless otherwise identified, all Scripture quotations in this publication are taken from the *New American Standard Bible* (NASB), © The Lockman Foundation 1960, 1962, 1963, 1968, 1971, 1972, 1973, 1975, 1977, 1995. Other versions used include: the HOLY BIBLE: NEW INTERNATIONAL VERSION® (NIV®). Copyright © 1973, 1978, 1984 by International Bible Society. Used by permission of Zondervan Publishing House. All rights reserved; THE MESSAGE (MSG). Copyright © 1993, 1994, 1995, 1996, 2000, 2001, 2002. Used by permission of NavPress Publishing Group; *The Living Bible* (TLB), Copyright © 1971, used by permission of Tyndale House Publishers, Inc., Wheaton, IL 60189, all rights reserved; and the *King James Version* (KJV).

Library of Congress Cataloging-in-Publication Data
Sandin, Fran Caffey, 1942-
  Touching the clouds : encouraging stories to make your faith soar /
Fran Caffey Sandin.
     p. cm.
Includes bibliographical references.
  ISBN 1-57683-341-0
  1. Christian life. I. Title.
  BV4501.3.S26 2003
  242--dc21
                              2003000357
Printed in the United States of America

1 2 3 4 5 6 7 8 9 10 / 07 06 05 04 03

FOR A FREE CATALOG OF
NAVPRESS BOOKS & BIBLE STUDIES,
CALL 1-800-366-7788 (USA)
OR 1-416-499-4615 (CANADA)

It is with deep love and appreciation that I dedicate this book to my mother, Billie Frances Caffey. Her example of steadfast faith through many trials has inspired me, my family, and countless others. I am thankful for this beautiful woman of God who has greatly influenced my life through her guidance and prayers. Mother, you are a blessing!

Contents

ACKNOWLEDGMENTS

I'd like to thank the women who have courageously granted me permission to write their stories. Each one has been a catalyst to strengthen my own faith, and I pray the "living water" they discovered will flow from the following pages into the heart of every reader. Thanks to my writer friends and authors who have encouraged me to the finish line: Gracie Malone, Becky Freeman, Susan Duke, Rebecca Jordan, Brenda Waggoner, Kali Schneiders, Jane Jarrell, Karol Ladd, and Jan Winebrenner. I'm grateful, too, for the support of other members in the Advanced Writers and Speakers Association (AWSA).

If you have ever prayed for me, please accept my deepest appreciation! Special thanks to my Monday night prayer partners: Carol Lawson, Judy Shaver, Karen Mayo, Patty Hendricks, Nancy Wight, Linda Cardwell, and Carolyn Johnson. Without your prayers and those of dear friends Linda Gilbert, Sandra Oliver, and others, this book would not be cradled in your hands today.

My heartfelt thanks to acquisitions editor Nanci McAlister for sharing my vision for this book, and also to my talented editor, Greg Clouse, who helped me focus and add the finishing touches. It has been great working with the NavPress staff!

My husband, Jim, deserves a standing ovation. He calls himself a "patron of the arts" and has gone the extra mile to be supportive and helpful, enriching me with his insights and allowing me more time to write. I consider myself fortunate and very blessed that you are my husband, Jim. I love you.

To my children and grandchildren: "Mimi" appreciates your love, prayers, and cheerful support. (Now I'll bake that batch of cookies!)

This verse expresses my heart: "Not to us, O Lord, not to us but *to your name be the glory*, because of your love and faithfulness" (Psalm 115:1, NIV, emphasis added).

INTRODUCTION

When crisis comes and emotions crumble, questions multiply. We may ask: "How can I cope?" "What next?" "God, where are You?" Through the years I have been acquainted with women who have asked similar questions. Their lives impacted mine because of their response to unexpected events. Some women had searched for meaning in all the wrong places before giving their hearts to Christ. Others struggled with obeying God in a certain matter. A few remembered the principles of faith and inspired others. Still others cried out to God in their distress. Yet even when God was silent, they made a decision to trust His heart and to believe His Word.

Touching the Clouds shows how exercising biblical faith really does make a difference. It challenges the reader to strengthen her own faith, encouraging her to stand firm, whatever her situation may be.

Popular recording artist Cynthia Clawson once said, "I have always been enamored with the first chapter of 2 Corinthians. Paul talks about the common sufferings and the common consolations that we share. I know this is true. When I know someone else survived an experience, and I find myself in a similar situation, I feel that I can survive, too."[1]

Is faith enough? What is faith? Why do we need it? Where do we find it? Faith is not something we can handle and touch, yet its results are plainly evident. Its main elements include:

Believing that Scripture is God's truth,
holding onto His truth relentlessly,
surrendering our lives to Christ, and
conducting ourselves accordingly.

Our faith walk begins when we believe in God's character and trust Him. But when trials and testings come—and they will, according to James 1—what is our response?

"Dwight L. Moody described three kinds of faith in Jesus Christ:

struggling faith, which is like a man in deep water;
clinging faith, which is like a man hanging to the side of
the boat; and
resting faith, which finds a man safely within the boat and
able moreover to reach out with a hand to help someone
else."[2]

While the women I interviewed are graciously sharing their lives as a way of reaching out, each of us determines our own response to life and its trials and what kind of faith we'll demonstrate. Faith grows with exercise. When body muscles are idle, they become flabby and weak. In a similar way, if we become spiritually lax, we rely upon our feelings rather than upon God's Word and so become discouraged. Just as a good workout builds healthier bodies, exercising faith is oxygen for the soul.

The "Faithlifter" at the end of each chapter is designed to help you to exercise your faith and apply it to daily living. Each "Faithlifter" is divided into three sections:

- In Her Shoes
- In His Word
- In Your Life

Through them you'll connect another woman's story to your own, find strength in the Scriptures, and begin to nurture an important characteristic of faith for the rest of your journey. And remember, you do not walk alone. I am holding your hand, walking alongside you on this faith journey, because, like you, *I have not yet arrived.* However, I am excited about our final destination and about what we can both learn along the way.

"And without faith it is impossible to please Him, for he who comes to God must believe that He is, and that He is a rewarder of those who seek Him" (Hebrews 11:6).

In the Bible, clouds are always connected with God. Clouds are those sorrows or sufferings without or within our personal lives which seem to dispute the empire of God. Seen apart from God, the clouds or difficulties are accidents, but when seen as from the Spirit of God they become our teachers which show us how to walk by faith.

—Oswald Chambers

CHAPTER ONE

Learning Unconditional Love

*Judy Anderson**

My husband, John, and I were stunned as our daughter told us that for years she had been struggling with a serious eating disorder. Corine had always been a delightful, compliant child. Through the years I thought I'd done everything right as a parent. Now we couldn't believe what she was telling us.

"But Mama, you don't understand!" Corine insisted with a quivering voice. Her piercing blue eyes pled for help as she spoke. Shoulder-length blonde hair softly framed her tear-stained face.

"No, Corine, I don't understand," I said. "But I'm trying."

The thought of my twenty-two-year-old daughter having an eating disorder was beyond my comprehension. Bulimia—characterized by bouts of overeating followed by voluntary vomiting, fasting, or induced diarrhea—disgusted me. I didn't want to talk about it.

Because Corine appeared healthy, her circumstances were even more difficult to grasp. Yet somehow we had failed to hear her silent cries.

*Judy Anderson is a pseudonym.

In a few weeks, Corine's university classmates would graduate, but she would not be among them. Her caring roommates tried to help Corine with her problem, but when their efforts failed, they said, "Corine, you must tell your parents, or we will." Courageously, Corine had come home.

My initial response was denial. A nightmare supplanted my fairy-tale dreams for Corine's future. *How could Corine do this to us?* I thought. We seemed to be a good Christian family. She'd attended a Christian high school and gone to church regularly. We'd given her a comfortable home.

As a perfectionist, I thought that if I were a diligent parent, Corine would grow up and live happily ever after. I often prayed, "Lord, if I love You and serve You, I know You'll make everything right." Deep in my heart I just knew He would honor my efforts. Now I was upset with not only Corine, but also God. *How could He let this happen?*

After the initial jolt of Corine's disclosure, John and I consulted our pastor and several mature Christians, who recommended that we send Corine to a professional counselor. But I realized I needed help, too. I began to pray fervently, "Please, Lord, give me understanding."

After one counseling session, Corine came home and said, "I'm so relieved to be talking with the counselor, but it just kills me to see you and Daddy hurting so much." The counselor had reminded her, "You've been working through this for four years, Corine, but your parents are just now beginning."

Touched by her concern, I looked at Corine and reassured her, "Your daddy and I will bounce back from this."

My emotional anguish continued, however, as I tried to sort out new developments. Throughout her weeks of counseling, I kept recalling Corine's teen years, when she occasionally made statements such as, "I hate myself," or "Why do I keep memorizing Scriptures and sinning like crazy?" Her words now echoed in my memory.

As time passed, I realized Corine did not need my preaching or judgmental attitudes—she craved my love and encouragement. It sounded easy, but demonstrating unconditional love was difficult.

My first opportunity came soon after Corine moved back home. At first it seemed awkward having her back in her old room. I'd forgotten that while she was away, I'd used some of her drawer space for storage.

One night, I went up to Corine's room to get some wallpaper samples from one of the drawers. When I opened the dresser, my heart sank. The drawer was filled with boxes of assorted chocolates. I closed the drawer quickly and went downstairs to the dark, quiet family room to talk with God.

"O Lord, she is our only daughter. Have mercy," I prayed. I didn't know what else to do.

Later that evening, I walked by Corine's bedroom door. Seeing that I was upset, Corine asked, "Mama, what's wrong?"

Stepping inside, I said, "Corine, I would never infringe upon your privacy, but tonight I opened the top dresser drawer to get some wallpaper samples."

Her countenance fell. I could see in her eyes that she knew I had discovered the chocolates.

Remembering that Corine liked butterflies, I remarked, "Maybe some butterflies just need more food than other butterflies." That was all I said. I felt the firm restraint of God's grace upon me as I pleasantly whispered good night, gave her a hug, and went to bed.

The next morning as Corine and I drove along in the car, she quietly said, "Mama, last night you reminded me of a Scripture: 'God's kindness leads you toward repentance' (Romans 2:4, NIV). Last night *your* kindness led me to repentance. After you went to bed, I got down on my knees and cleaned out my heart. Then I got up off my knees and cleaned out my drawer."

"I'm proud of you, Corine," I said. Silently, I thanked God for the victory in both our lives.

A godly woman had recently advised me to use the "zipped-lip principle." My former tendency would have been to launch into a lengthy sermon. But through the power of the Holy Spirit, I refrained. He taught me that "love is kind" (1 Corinthians 13:4) and that sometimes kindness means silence.

From Corine's counselor I learned that those who are caught in bulimia's trap sometimes gravitate to drug abuse, alcoholism, immorality, or kleptomania. About two weeks later, an unexpected telephone call revealed that our daughter also had further struggles.

When I answered the phone, Corine cried, "Mama," and then wept.

"Corine, what's the matter?" I said. "Everything will be all right."

"No, it won't," she answered between sobs. "I was caught stealing five cans of tuna. The police walked me out of the grocery store after the manager called them. My car is in the pound. I've been fingerprinted and a mug shot's been taken."

I felt numb. Yet I continued to inwardly beg, *Lord, please help me understand.*

It was her second arrest. This time a judge placed her on probation with the stipulation that if she were caught stealing in the next six months, she would go directly to prison.

Six weeks after her probation began, Corine and I spent an evening together and talked about her kleptomania. Nervously, I reached for the cross dangling from my necklace, sliding it back and forth on the chain. Corine had given it to me on Mother's Day.

"Mama, I even stole the necklace you're wearing," she said. My heart pounded as she quickly added, "But I've been good these past two weeks. I haven't stolen anything."

Lord, please help me say the right words, I silently prayed. We both knew the consequences if she were caught.

"Corine, I can't bear to think about you going to prison," I whispered.

"Mama, it gives me cold chills just to think about it," she confessed.

Afterward, I went downstairs and wept and prayed for hours. Broken, humiliated, silent, I turned to Jeremiah 17:7: "But blessed is the man who trusts in the Lord, whose confidence is in him" (NIV). Then I confessed to God that in the past I had trusted in my own efforts. I asked Him to be my trust, my bank account, from which I could draw love, courage, strength, wisdom, and grace. Next I read Psalm 62:5: "My soul, wait thou only upon God; for my expectation is from him" (KJV).

Taking a sheet of paper, I wrote out all my expectations concerning Corine:

- Having a mother-daughter friendship
- Being able to enjoy her wedding and her children
- Seeing her find fulfillment in her home life
- Delighting in seeing her serve the Lord
- Rejoicing in having a daughter who honors us with a godly life
- Gaining respect from being viewed as a good mother

My honest prayer became, "What do I ask, Lord? How does it make You feel? Did I injure her as her mother? You heal, You bind up, You set free. Do I have the right to ask You to keep her out of prison? I give it all up to You. Have mercy on me, a sinner. Please Lord, change me." Then I gave the list to God and said, "She's yours."

As morning dawned I was still awake, but my weariness was overshadowed by the excitement of God's grace. His message to me was, "Just love her."

I stepped into my dressing room, ran a comb through my hair, put on fresh lipstick, and went back into the kitchen to prepare a breakfast tray for Corine. I'd never done that before. It was a pretty white-wicker bed tray, complete with cloth napkin and butterfly holder, a fresh flower, and Corine's favorite foods.

I took the tray upstairs to Corine's room. She had just awakened. As I stood there, smiling, she burst into tears and said, "Mama, I've always thought that God is a God of wrath, but now I know that God is a God of love."

She stretched out her arms as I set down the tray. We hugged and cried together. I realized God was at work, and the less I said, the more clearly Corine could hear Him. As time passed, I became even more aware that God was changing me. As I "let go" of

Corine, she opened up to me. She began expressing her fears. I began confessing my faults. We began to laugh together. Gradually, we became transparent.

Eight years have passed since Corine revealed her battle with bulimia. She has made tremendous progress. In spite of her many heartaches, she finished college, was released from probation, held a job, married a wonderful man, and became the mother of two children.

Through this time, I learned that regardless of how hard the situation, God always meets us at our point of need. By His grace it is never too late to restore a damaged relationship.

Christian psychologist and author H. Norman Wright encouraged me with these words:

> You have failed in the past. You are failing now in some way. You will fail in the future. You weren't perfect in the past. You won't be perfect in the future. Your children will not be perfect, either. When you fail, allow yourself to feel disappointment, but not disapproval. When you release your grip on perfectionism, the fear of failure will release its grip on you. You can fail and not be a failure![1]

Overcoming perfectionism has been a painful process, but I feel God urging me to leave the past behind and to keep looking ahead (see Philippians 3:12-14). I've adopted a healthier goal: not seeking perfection, but seeking to become more like the Perfect One, Jesus Christ, and loving others unconditionally, the way He loves me.

Faithlifter

Love

IN HER SHOES

Judy had to wait for God to work in her daughter's life, and in the meantime, Judy learned more about God's love for them both as He met each at her individual point of need. Isn't it great to know that God loves us as we are and that He loves us so much He keeps moving us to a higher spiritual plane?

Judy struggled to "let go" of her expectations and place her daughter in God's hands. Can you identify with her dilemma? Judy reached a turning point when she realized she could not change Corine, but could change her own attitudes. Have you ever been challenged in a similar way? Have you extended unconditional love, only to have the other person reject you? What happened then?

Exercising love is not just having a mushy, soft feeling; it is doing what is best for the object of that love and leaving that person's response in the Lord's hands. Sometimes it involves confrontation while other times it means staying quiet and prayerful while God weaves His Word into the fibers of our souls. Human love will often fail, but God's love never fails. As Judy learned, our goal is to become like Him, the One who is love.

IN HIS WORD

In the Creation account recorded in Genesis 1–2, we see how God lovingly prepared for mankind. As a family readies the house for a new baby, outfits the nursery, and prepares the crib, God, in His awesome, incomprehensible power, prepared the universe for man. Then He made man in His own image, each unique person with the capability to love but also with the ability to choose. After Adam and Eve disobeyed God and chose to sin, God kept reaching out in sacrificial love. Again, He provided. Throughout Scripture we see God's merciful, forgiving, restoring, sacrificial, unfailing love.

God is love.

Love expresses the very nature of God. It should also characterize God's children in our attitudes toward one another. *Agape* and *agapao*, the Greek words for love in the New Testament, are used to explain the attitude of God toward His Son, the human race in general, and particularly those who believe in the Lord Jesus Christ.

"Dear friends, let us love one another, for love comes from God. Everyone who loves has been born of God and knows God. Whoever does not love does not know God, because God is love" (1 John 4:7-8, NIV).

Love is the attribute of God that is sometimes the most difficult to reconcile in our finite human understanding. We look at tragedies and ask, *If God is a God of love, why did He let this terrible thing happen? God—how could You?* We look at people we don't like and ask, *How can I love him? How can I love her?* And yet our definition of love is so limited that we fail to see the whole picture of who God is and what He has done.

God demonstrated His love.

"This is how God showed his love among us: He sent his one and only Son into the world that we might live through him. This is love: not that we loved God, but that he loved us and sent his Son as an atoning sacrifice for our sins" (1 John 4:9-10, NIV).

"This is how we know what love is: Jesus Christ laid down his life for us. And we ought to lay down our lives for our brothers" (1 John 3:16, NIV).

The apostle Paul indicated that the love of God is beyond human comprehension. But he prayed the Ephesians would "grasp how wide and long and high and deep is the love of Christ, and to know this love that surpasses knowledge—that [they] may be filled to the measure of all the fullness of God" (Ephesians 3:18-19, NIV).

God expects us to love Him.

The Pharisees asked, "'Teacher, which is the greatest commandment in the Law?'

"Jesus replied: 'Love the Lord your God with all your heart and with all your soul and with all your mind.' This is the first and greatest commandment. And the second is like it: 'Love your neighbor as yourself'" (Matthew 22:36-39, NIV).

God expects us to love others.

Unlike Hollywood love, Christian love toward fellow believers or toward others in general does not spring from an impulse of feelings or a special affinity. It acts in obedience to Scripture (see 1 Corinthians 13; Colossians 3:12-14) and is not self-centered but seeks to please God. Showing love helps the undeserving to see the Holy Spirit at work and helps us reverence God, who initiates that kind of love for each one of us.

As the familiar chorus says, "They will know we are Christians by our love."

IN YOUR LIFE

Just as God demonstrated His love for us while we were sinners (see Romans 5:8), He calls on us to verify love in practical ways. Suppose someone has offended you many times and personality conflicts hinder your relationship. These suggestions may help:

- Say a kind word to her or do a nice deed for her, even if you don't feel like it.
- Make a small gift (bread, cookies, or a craft item) and give it as a surprise.
- As you prepare your gift, pray for her, "Lord, you know I cannot love in my own strength. So I ask that You would simply use me as a channel for Your love. Let me know how You want to love through me."
- Remember that you are responsible to love, but the other person's response is out of your control.

- Meditate on 1 Corinthians 13:4-8, using different Bible translations. Pray the Lord will continue to help you understand biblical love and practice it. Through a personal relationship with Christ, we grasp the meaning of unconditional love. This love sparks the birth of a new process in our lives—Christian growth with the development of the fruit of the Spirit (see Galatians 5:22-23).

Dr. Dwight Pentecost wrote: "Love for God produces obedience. The way to please God is to have a heart that is set on Him. And a heart that is set on Him obeys His commands. Obedience manifests itself when we love others."[2]

Mother Teresa once said, "If faith is scarce, it is because there is too much selfishness in the world, too much egoism. Faith, in order to be authentic, has to be generous and giving. Love and faith go hand in hand."[3]

During life's trials, we can rest assured that God loves us. Nothing we do can make Him love us more. Nothing we do can make Him love us less. His love is unchanging, unfailing, everlasting.

CHAPTER TWO

Are You Kidding, God?

Allyson Neighbors

I noticed her as I hurried past the open door—the door to a condom store. My Bible study meeting at the student union had dismissed at 9:30 that chilly fall night. The campus surrounded me, dark and deserted. I could hardly wait to find my parked car and return to the warmth and security of my dorm.

Two doors farther down the sidewalk, the girl's image was still imprinted in my mind. She sat on a stool behind the counter. Perhaps it was her drooping shoulders that caught my attention, or the jet-black hair partly blocking her face from view. Then it came. A thought? An inner voice?

Witness to the girl.

Was I imagining things? Witness to someone in a condom store? What would my friends think? I shivered and pulled my coat tight around me, wondering what I should do.

Okay, Lord. I'll drive around the block. If she's standing—not sitting—when I drive by, I'll go in.

With a feeling of relief, I hurried to my car and slipped the key into the door lock. I got behind the wheel and slammed the door, locking it almost in the same motion. I hoped the girl would still be seated as I drove my car from the parking lot and eased slowly in front of the store. But she was standing, her pretty face clearer now.

She's standing! Now what do I do? I let the car roll ahead, trying to decide. *Lord, I have to be sure! I'll circle the block. If she's still standing, then I'll go inside.* I barely accelerated, turned right again, and once more. My heart pounded as I saw her again, standing at the counter and staring into the night outside.

I took a deep breath and said a quick prayer as I parked the car. Stepping out, I lifted my head, fixed my smile in place, and marched through the shop's open door. The girl turned to face me.

"Hi!" I said brightly. "My name is Allyson. I was, uh, just driving by and . . . well, uh, I felt I should come inside to meet you."

"Hi," she said, her voice friendly but puzzled. "I'm Becky."

"Are you a student?" I asked, noticing that her deep brown eyes appeared to be slightly red and swollen.

"Yes, a freshman," she sighed. "First semester. How about you?"

"I'm a sophomore," I answered, beginning to relax. "I remember last year and the adjustments I had to make. First year away from home in such a big school."

"You know," she said, her eyes searching mine, "it's really weird you came in. I've been crying all evening. I've been having problems with my boyfriend." She paused, then added, "I've decided to see a psychiatrist in the morning."

"Well, I had different kinds of problems my freshman year, but my parents were a big help—really supportive. They helped me see that even if I mess up in school, it's not the end of the world. Jesus will be there for me no matter how bad things may seem."

Becky explained, "My dad's from India. He's a Muslim. My mother was a member of a Protestant church, but when she married my dad, the people in the church disowned her. She never went back." Becky hesitated, and then added, "Our family never went to church." She said it as if that disqualified her from having any right to call on God now.

"Becky," I said, feeling it would be all right with her for me to go on, "you may not have a church background, but you can know the reality of God in your life. Jesus can turn your life around. He loves you. He wants to be your friend."

She bowed her head, and her long hair fell forward, hiding her face from me again. I had the feeling the conversation was over. I dared to touch her shoulder. "I'll be praying for you," I said softly. "Maybe this tract will help to answer some of your questions. My name and phone number are on the back. I hope you'll call me." As I turned and walked toward the door, I heard her speak quietly.

"I might call you sometime."

Looking back I responded, "Please do," putting all the warmth I could into my voice.

Stepping into the crisp night air, I felt like skipping to the car. Exuberantly I thought, *Lord, if You are bringing her to Yourself, thank You for letting me in on Your plan. I can't wait to see what You're going to do.*

Several months passed. I prayed for Becky occasionally, and then forgot about her until the spring. One day as I walked past the condom store, I glanced inside and saw her. On an impulse, I went in, hoping no one had seen me.

"Allyson," Becky exclaimed. "I remember you! You came in that night I was so upset. You really seemed to care about me."

Then she enthusiastically updated me on her life. "After you came in, some girls in my dorm invited me to a Bible study, and I went. When I told them I was worried about an upcoming test, they asked if they could pray for me. Allyson," she said, her eyes twinkling, "no one had ever prayed for me before, and they prayed for me!"

By this time, I was smiling. "And you remember the boyfriend I told you about? I'm not seeing him anymore."

Becky's transparent confession reassured me that God had been preparing her for our encounter. After we chatted a few more minutes, I found an appropriate pause and said, "Becky, Jesus loves you and wants to come into your heart, but He will not barge in. You have to open the door. Jesus said, 'Behold, I stand at the door and knock; if anyone hears My voice and opens the door, I will come in to him, and will dine with him, and he with Me' (Revelation 3:20)."

Becky nodded her head and seemed to be trying to comprehend. We parted on a cordial note and I promised to keep in touch.

Later, I learned that the following Sunday, Becky attended church for the first time with the girls at the dorm who had prayed for her. And the first thing she noticed was a stained glass window depicting Jesus knocking on the door, with the verse from Revelation 3:20 printed below.

The next time I saw Becky, she told me, "Allyson, when I saw that picture of Jesus, I understood what you were talking about. For the first time, I felt a nudge inside me. Oh, I can't explain it—I just knew that Jesus wanted to come in. And I said yes! Now I just want to do everything I can to be more like Him."

Whoa! I felt so excited. Becky had no preconceived notions about God, so she jumped right into Bible study with a teachable heart. As she daily read God's Word, Becky became more patient, understanding, and kind.

Several weeks later her roommate, Amy, asked Becky, "What has happened to you?" When Becky described the events leading up to her new life in Christ, Amy decided that, though she had been a church member for many years, she did not know the Savior. So she also prayed to receive Jesus.

As I led both women through a six-week discipleship course, my own faith was encouraged. Becky accompanied me as I witnessed on campus during an evangelistic emphasis week. We all experienced answered prayer after we prayed for Amy's grandfather, who had moved to the city and felt lonely without family nearby. The following week, Amy talked with her grandfather and learned that someone had visited him every day—not just one day, but every day.

Becky quit her job at the condom store and began working at a restaurant. Today she is a radiant believer who eagerly shares her faith and continues seeking Christian growth and fellowship. Before meeting Becky, I had asked God to use me to share His love, and He certainly did not disappoint.

Faithlifter
Courage

IN HER SHOES

When Allyson felt that still, small voice tugging at her heart to witness to the girl in the condom store, she was reluctant to obey because the situation made her uncomfortable. Have you ever had a similar experience? However, when Allyson chose to obey God's inner prompting, her caring conversation impressed Becky.

Allyson did not know at the time that others were concerned about and praying for Becky, but her encounter became a crucial link in the chain of events that ultimately led to Becky's salvation. We may not always understand why God is leading in a certain direction, but often it is because He wants us to participate in His bigger picture.

Have you ever stopped to think about the long-lasting and far-reaching impact of one courageous act?

IN HIS WORD

Moses had followed God in leading the people of Israel toward the Promised Land, but after Moses had died and the time of mourning had passed, Joshua became the leader. God must have known that Joshua's knees were knocking when He gave him these words:

> "Be strong and courageous, for you shall give this people possession of the land which I swore to their fathers to give them. Only be strong and very courageous; be careful to do according to all the law which Moses My servant commanded you; do not turn from it to the right or to the left, so that you may have success wherever you go. This book of the law shall not depart from your mouth, but you shall meditate on it day and night, so that you may be careful to

do according to all that is written in it; for then you will make your way prosperous, and then you will have success. Have I not commanded you? Be strong and courageous! Do not tremble or be dismayed, for the Lord your God is with you wherever you go." (Joshua 1:6-9)

Joshua was following God's leading, but it appeared that God was taking him toward danger. After all, they needed to cross the Jordan River before reaching Canaan. How would they get to the other side? God gave specific directions. When the priests stepped into the water, it rolled back like a wall, and the priests stood holding the Ark of the Covenant while the people walked across the dry riverbed into the Promised Land. God had delivered them!

The following verses have reminded me of God's presence when I have been afraid instead of courageous:

"Do not fear, for I have redeemed you; I have called you by name; you are Mine!" (Isaiah 43:1).

"For God hath not given us the spirit of fear; but of power, and of love, and of a sound mind" (2 Timothy 1:7, KJV).

"He Himself has said, 'I will never desert you, nor will I ever forsake you,' so that we confidently say, 'The Lord is my helper, I will not be afraid. What shall man do to me?'" (Hebrews 13:5-6).

IN YOUR LIFE

God does not want us to whine when He calls us to a seemingly impossible task. He is already on the other side and knows the rest of the story. He doesn't want us to make excuses or point toward someone else who, in our opinion, could do a job better. I think He is saying, "Be the best you can be. Go, and be strong in the Lord."

Here are some ideas that may help you exercise courage:

- Be alert. Remember that Satan, our adversary, wants to drag you into the ditch of discouragement.
- Be transparent and confess your fears to God. He understands.

- Pray for boldness and confidence. As one pastor said, "Courage is fear that has said its prayers."
- Memorize Scriptures, say the verses aloud, and make positive confessions.
- Set your sights on the goal. Look beyond the immediate circumstance toward the goal you wish to accomplish.
- Remember that God is for you.

God does not always remove obstacles, but He gives us strength to face them. With each victorious encounter, faith will grow.

I heard a taped message once by Corrie ten Boom in which she expressed it this way:

"Look outward and be distressed,
Look inward and be depressed,
Look upward and be at rest."

"Am I waiting for God to increase my faith so that I'll have the courage to obey, or am I asking God for the courage to obey so that He can increase my faith?"[1]

CHAPTER THREE

God Sent an Angel

Sherry Latimer

Tingling with excitement, I dressed our infant daughter, Kelly, in ruffles and lace. Mother's Day was designated as Baby Dedication Day at church, and for the first time, I would be recognized with the other moms. I could hardly wait! To top off the morning, my husband, Doug, smiled and, with a twinkle in his eye, kissed me on the cheek while placing an orchid corsage in my hand. I felt like a queen.

The thrilling day met all my expectations. On Mother's Day five years later, I felt the same sense of anticipation as I clothed our infant son, Daniel. Doug cherished his boy. A sense of accomplishment prevailed as I stood with the other mothers during the worship service. A few years later, though, everything changed.

When I was seven months along in a third pregnancy, I became concerned. Our baby seemed lethargic. I mentioned my anxiety to the doctor when I saw him for a regular checkup. But after finding a strong heartbeat, he remarked, "You're probably carrying a dainty little girl."

Because Doug and I are both tall, we didn't expect to have a tiny baby. But perhaps the doctor was right. Maybe this baby was just smaller than the others had been. We even joked about it and tried to accept his explanation.

But I couldn't shake the feeling that something was wrong. At home after my checkup, I noticed several magazine articles describing complications during pregnancy. Why hadn't I been aware of these things before? Was God trying to prepare me for a catastrophe? Why was I so upset?

The more I pondered my pregnancy and the unfamiliar symptoms I was experiencing, the more nagging questions alarmed me. Then one day I discussed my fears with Doug.

"Honey, I know the doctor said not to worry, but I really think something is wrong with this baby."

"Sherry," Doug said with in an understanding tone, "if you feel so strongly about this, I'll call the doctor myself. Maybe he needs to check you again."

"Oh, please do. Thank you so much." I felt the security of Doug's decisiveness and protectiveness as we embraced.

When Doug called Dr. Allen, it was suggested we return to the hospital for further tests. Near the appointed time, I felt apprehensive. But that day, friendly nurses eased my tension by explaining each step of the extensive examination, including a sonogram and amniocentesis.

The test results affirmed my greatest fears. Dr. Allen discovered that our baby had life-threatening defects in both her brain and other vital organs. "I'm sorry to have to tell you this, but I want to prepare you for the possibility that your baby may be stillborn."

I sobbed all the way home. All I could think about was the baby and our disappointment. Doug was hurting, too, but his strong, masculine stability comforted me. For weeks I cried. My thoughts were a series of questions: *Would I give birth to a deformed baby girl? How would this affect our other children? Would our baby be born dead?*

The day my labor began, I was caught up in my own world of

thought, prayer, and anguish. Although loving parents, siblings, and church friends reassured us of their concern, I had to walk through this crisis myself. No one could do it for me. In my heart I was crying out, "God, are You there?"

Childbirth, a happy time for most couples, became mournful. Our daughter was stillborn. The nurses wrapped her in a blanket and covered her anencephalic head so that all we could see was her beautiful face. Doug and I named her Angel René. Through our tears, we knew that somehow God could use our experience for good, but at the time, the pain was too blinding. For a while, nothing could ease the lonely, forsaken, empty feeling in my soul.

Our pastor came to the hospital to be with us in our loss and to pray with and for us. A private burial service facilitated our grief and illustrated to our older children, Kelly and Daniel, the sacredness of Angel's life. Friends reached out in loving ways, but for me, life seemed to stop.

As the weeks and months passed, I struggled spiritually. I knew that Angel was with the Lord, without deformity. However, her death left me with many puzzling questions.

Because I grew up in a Christian home and most of my prayers had been answered in a way that pleased me, I just couldn't understand why Angel died. I worried that God had decided I was an unfit mother. Then I compared myself with other moms who didn't seem to spend time with their children. As an elementary teacher, I enjoyed little ones. It didn't seem right for God to let my baby die. On and on like a merry-go-round I rehashed events, chastened myself, and kept wondering . . . *why?*

The following Mother's Day was one of the most painful days of my life. I didn't even want to go to church. I felt like others were judging me, even though I knew it wasn't true. Reluctantly, I dressed to go.

During the baby dedication time, I should have been standing in front of the congregation holding our new daughter. Instead, I sat in the pew with empty arms and a broken heart. Seeing the other happy moms with their babies made me angry and bitter. I couldn't even sense a oneness of spirit with my own mother because she had never experienced the death of a child. Although she tried to understand, she was bewildered by my grief. I wanted to withdraw from everyone, and for a time, I did.

In quiet times, I reflected on various events, including my awful Mother's Day. Even though I had been consumed with myself, I recalled several friends who had acknowledged my heart-wrenching moments. They had hugged me, complimented my appearance, and with their eyes let me know they remembered it was my first Mother's Day since Angel's death. Several women had lifted my spirits by saying, "I'm praying for you." I needed to hear those words. Gradually, warm feelings began to thaw the cold shell I'd wrapped around myself.

As I opened my Bible once again, I began studying about people who had faced trials. The Holy Spirit opened my eyes to new truths. When reading about God telling Abraham to sacrifice his son Isaac, I understood. Abraham obeyed God because Abraham was looking beyond the promise that his descendants would multiply. He trusted the Promise-maker. God provided a ram for the sacrifice and kept His promise to Abraham. The lamb was a picture of Jesus. For the first time, I realized that through Jesus, God had provided for me, too. Not only was He comforting me, but He was comforting Angel as well.

Then I looked through the Psalms and identified with David's struggles. He had doubts, too. "How long, O Lord? Will you forget me forever? How long will you hide your face from me?" (Psalm 13:1, NIV). But through God's grace David apparently found relief. "I trust in your unfailing love; my heart rejoices in your salvation. I will sing to the Lord, for he has been good to me" (verses 5-6, NIV).

Like David, I began to recount the ways God had been good. Through the Christlike behavior of my friends, through their attentiveness, through a supportive husband and answered prayer, I realized that Jesus had not forsaken me. In fact, I felt humbled to acknowledge the many ways He had cared for me. Focusing on Him instead of my pain, I gained a new perspective of salvation through Christ and its far-reaching implications.

I found help in Jerry Bridges' book, *Trusting God: Even When Life Hurts*, in which he states, "We usually find within ourselves reasons why we think God should NOT love us. Such searching is unbiblical. The Bible is quite clear that God does not look within us for a reason to love us. He loves us because we are in Christ Jesus. God's love to us cannot fail any more than His love to Christ can fail."[1]

He continues, "It is just as important to trust God as it is to obey Him. When we disobey God we defy His authority and despise His holiness. But when we fail to trust God we doubt His sovereignty and question His goodness. In both cases we cast aspersions upon His majesty and character."[2]

I began to understand that whatever calamity happens in our lives, God always knows what is best because He has infinite wisdom and perfect love. Only through Scripture could I gain the faith I needed to trust our sovereign God.

After three years—through the help of my friends, family, prayer, and Bible study—God has lit my dark pit of despair and brought me to greater maturity in Him. I've become more sensitive to others in their time of emotional need. I appreciate my children more, realizing how precious each life is to God. My faith is deeper now, knowing that even when I felt like forsaking God, He kept His promises to me. He has replaced my sadness with joy. Yes, I too, am learning to trust God, even when life hurts.

Once again I'm looking forward to Mother's Day. For one thing, we will dedicate our beautiful, new, healthy daughter, Julie, to the Lord. But most of all, I will praise God for sending Angel. She helped me learn the real difference between happiness and joy.

"Weeping may endure for a night, but joy cometh in the morning" (Psalm 30:5, KJV).

Faithlifter
Gentleness

IN HER SHOES

Perhaps you have experienced a similar loss—a miscarriage or still-born baby. How does Sherry's experience compare? Having experienced two miscarriages as well as the death of a seventeen-month-old son, I can certainly identify with Sherry's feelings of loss and isolation. Grief is a lonely road we each walk at some time or another, but not by ourselves. I learned, just as Sherry discovered, that our tender Shepherd holds our hand and walks beside us down the stony path. He knows we are lonely, but He reassures us we are not alone.

Gentleness means we do not try to rush in and "fix" grieving people with lots of Bible verses, judgmental observations, and unrealistic expectations. We can be with them, listen, cry with them, encourage them with our presence and our prayers, and love them unconditionally. A Christlike spirit of gentleness is a powerful witness any time, but is especially meaningful to the grieving.

IN HIS WORD

Our culture often associates *greatness* with aggressiveness and power, but David points to God's *gentleness* as the source of greatness. "Thou hast also given me the shield of Thy salvation: and Thy right hand hath holden me up, and Thy gentleness hath made me great. Thou hath enlarged my steps under me, that my feet did not slip" (Psalm 18:35-36, KJV).

When used as an adjective, the Greek word for *gentleness* indicates looking at a situation with forbearance. It denotes considerateness instead of contentiousness. Instead of insisting on the letter of the law, it means looking humanly and reasonably at the facts. In 1 Timothy 3:3, gentleness is listed among the qualities of an overseer or deacon: "not violent, but gentle, not quarrelsome"(NIV).

Paul refers to his conduct toward new converts in Thessalonica with these words: "As apostles of Christ we could have been a burden to you, but we were gentle among you, like a mother caring for her little children. We loved you so much that we were delighted to share with you not only the gospel of God but our lives as well, because you had become so dear to us" (1 Thessalonians 2:7-8, NIV).

Another Greek adjective for *gentleness* is translated "good, kind, easy, or gracious." It is used to describe Christ when Paul spoke in 2 Corinthians 10:1: "By the meekness and gentleness of Christ, I appeal to you" (NIV).

Gentleness is not always respected in our society, but it is love in action—having a teachable spirit, being considerate, placing the needs of others above our own. The selfishness that drives a carnal, domineering attitude can only be tamed by the work of the Holy Spirit, as described by Paul: "But when the Holy Spirit controls our lives he will produce this kind of fruit in us: love, joy, peace, patience, kindness, goodness, faithfulness, gentleness and self-control; and here there is no conflict with Jewish laws" (Galatians 5:22, TLB).

The gentle one allows Christ to comfort her: "Your adornment must not be merely external—braiding the hair, and wearing gold jewelry, or putting on dresses; but let it be the hidden person of the heart, with the imperishable quality of a gentle and quiet spirit, which is precious in the sight of God" (1 Peter 3:3-4).

IN YOUR LIFE

One of the most difficult things to do when people grieve is to allow them time to recover. In our drive-through-window society, we sometimes expect the family to drive home from the memorial service and resume normality, when, in reality, it takes time—months, sometimes even years—for emotions to heal.

I have found these practical suggestions helpful in ministering to a grieving mother:

- During the week prior to Mother's Day, offer to take your grieving friend to lunch, to a play, window-shopping, or to visit a museum or art gallery. The gift of your time is a great way to show God's love.

- Select an encouraging Mother's Day card and send it with a note, letting her know that she is a mother worthy of honor.

- Do not be afraid to mention the child who died, and when you do, be ready to listen patiently if the mother wishes to talk about the child.

- Write the dates of the child's birthday and death on your calendar. When those days are near, send a note or card letting your friend know you will be praying for her on that day. Pray for her.

- Make a list of verses that have encouraged you during your own trials and tests. Write one Scripture passage on a 3 x 5 card and share it with your friend.

- Acknowledge grieving children in the family by baking cookies just for them or giving them a small gift. Whatever you do for your friend's children will minister grace to her.

- Be available to help with practical needs such as running errands, helping with the laundry, or other household chores.

- If your bereaved friend has other children, offer to keep them one evening so she and her husband can have some time alone.

- Prepare a meal and deliver it in disposable containers.

- When you are with her, give her plenty of hugs.

Each of us has burdens from time to time. While it may not be the death of a child or a loved one, burdens come in many different forms. Our goal is to become a safe person, like Jesus — sensitive to the emotional, spiritual, and psychological needs of others.

The gentleness of Jesus makes Him approachable: "Come to me, all you who are weary and burdened, and I will give you rest. Take my yoke upon you and learn from me, for I am gentle and humble in heart, and you will find rest for your souls. For my yoke is easy and my burden is light" (Matthew 11:28-30, NIV).

CHAPTER FOUR

Standing in the Gap

Mable Dumas

In the spring of 1978 I attended a "Change the World School of Prayer" seminar, never dreaming the impact it would have in my life and in the lives of so many others. Dick Eastman, then president of World Literature Crusade, taught from a prayer wheel called "The Hour That Changes the World." It included several elements I had not used before in my devotional time, such as singing, meditation, and waiting.

Afterward I felt the Lord speaking to me through Matthew 26:40: "And He came to the disciples and found them sleeping and said to Peter, 'So, you men could not keep watch with me for one hour?'" It was as though He was calling me through His Word: "Mable, I want you to accept the challenge." The thought was so compelling that I committed to pray for one hour each day.

As a wife, mother, and Bible teacher, I spoke aloud: "Lord, I want to know You better, and because of that, I'm making an appointment for us to get together." I struggled with getting up an hour earlier each morning, so I decided to "report for duty" upon arising—turning my heart toward the Lord, asking for His guidance in my day—but our longer meeting took place later when I was at my best.

He and I began meeting out on my patio at first, away from the telephone and other interruptions. Initially, I wasn't sure how to address the Creator of the universe. It was a little awkward because I was trying too hard to be theologically correct, to use the right terms and say all the right words. It wore me out!

I strained to have an intimate relationship without it being either too religiously rigid or too casual, but as I got to know Him better, He became my Abba, my Daddy. Jesus said to address God as "Our Father." One day, like any caring parent, He said in my spirit, "Knock it off, Mable, I'm tired of this game, aren't you?" And I was.

How liberating when I finally dropped my pretenses and just exposed myself to Him, warts and all, and like a little child, experienced freedom in His presence. No longer was it a stiff, uncomfortable, ritualistic encounter. Instead it was as if I were walking with Jesus, holding His hand, and being transparent, totally honest, with nothing hidden.

Through concentrating upon His amazing love for me, I found it only natural to love and adore Him in return. Just to think that the mighty God, encased in humanity, had given Himself for me! My relationship became much more than just the time I spent during that hour. It became a "knowing" relationship that began bearing spiritual fruit. I never took lightly my promise to spend time with God, and if a hindering circumstance arose, I just talked it over with the Lord and planned another appointment.

Our meeting place changed a few years later when our pastor preached from Ezekiel 22:30: "I searched for a man among them who would build up the wall and stand in the gap before Me for the land, so that I would not destroy it; but I found no one." As a result, I placed a desk in my bedroom with a map of the world above it and designated it "The Gap." It quickly became hallowed ground as I met God there every day and prayed through my "lists," which included officials from the local school board and local government up to and including the Supreme Court. Another list consisted of leaders and members of my church. Yet another involved those needing salvation.

During vacation Bible school at our church, I set up an "Inspiration Corner" to pray for and encourage the staff, workers, and students. When I knew the gospel was being presented to a particular VBS group, I stood quietly outside the classroom door and prayed. During this time, I also began hosting a monthly prayer group in my home to help young women learn how to pray.

Does all this mean that I never had a problem? Hardly! My husband, Jack, and I taught young married couples in the church, but when our only son and his wife divorced, we were devastated. I couldn't even say the word *divorce*. I didn't have the power to change the situation, but I knew Someone who did. So I took up the armor of God and battled against the Evil One. I stood on the promises of God.

Believing that our daughter-in-law was meant to be in our family, I faithfully prayed for her return. As a result, fourteen months after their divorce, my son and his wife remarried with Christ at the center of their relationship. I also witnessed the blessing of their children—Stephanie, who died shortly after birth, and Jonathan, a bright, healthy son, now a teenager. When the remarriage first occurred, I told my friends, "They tried divorce, but it just didn't work out!"

During the sad and puzzling months of seemingly unanswered prayers, God uplifted me through phrases and Scriptures that I recorded on a flip-chart I called "Mind Programmers." I'm a visual person who loves bright colors, so I designed the charts and shared them with others; and now they have literally been sent around the world.

Here are a few Mind Programmers:

- Have the "tangles of life" got you all tied up? Then deposit these words into your consciousness: "Continue in prayer and watch in the same with thanksgiving" (based upon Colossians 4:2). That's a positive statement with no hidden clauses. So watch as He unravels the "tangles"!

- Don't bog down in your existing circumstances . . . climb up to your Christ! Refuse to allow circumstances to inhibit your believing!
- Prayer is not primarily getting my "want list" before the Lord. It is, first and foremost, getting "me" into His presence!
- God has no problems . . . only plans!
- This trial is not "by chance" but by divine permission!
- During trials and test, God puts you "center stage" and turns on the "spotlight," saying: "Let Me demonstrate and prove what I am in the life of this child of Mine!"

Anyone can be as close to God as he or she wants to be. He is willing and waiting. I use my divine imagination when reading Scripture and imagine myself running barefoot through the Psalms, finding words that speak of God's guidance, listening, answering, understanding, waiting, forgiving, watching. When I think of the Bible as words and thoughts from the mind of God, time spent with Him is always exciting, never boring. I have discovered that God doesn't want my day; He wants me.

Prayer also reminds us that we have Him. From *Faith's Checkbook*, by Charles Haddon Spurgeon, I read,

> On no one occasion will the Lord desert us. Happen what may, He will be at our side. Friends drop from us, their help is but an April shower; but God is faithful. Jesus is the same forever, and the Holy Spirit abideth in us.
>
> Come, my heart, be calm and hopeful today. Clouds may gather, but the Lord can blow them away. Since God will not fail me, my faith shall not fail; and as He will not forsake me, neither will I forsake Him. Oh, for a restful faith![1]

Faithlifter
Prayer

IN HER SHOES

Mable conversed with her heavenly Father with reverence and respect but also as she would her best friend. She demonstrated that prayer is not merely words, but a wonderful process that connects our hearts with His. Prayer is listening, concentrating, enlarging our understanding, and becoming more sensitive so we can fully trust Him. Have you also discovered these truths?

Prayer is talking with God and knowing that He is at work. Just as a seed germinates underground and we wait for the law of nature to push out the little sprout, God plants the seeds of His Word in our hearts, and as we keep tending, watering, and watching, an answer will soon come forth. On the days when Mable felt like nothing was happening, she continued praying and believing while God worked underground.

Do you ever feel like that you read your Bible and pray without seeing the results you expected? You can rest assured that He is working behind the scenes to conform you to the image of His Son and to strengthen you to receive His answer, whatever it may be.

IN HIS WORD

It is clear from Scripture that prayer and faith walk hand in hand. We are urged to "pray without ceasing" (1 Thessalonians 5:17). For the believer, prayer is not optional; it is essential to maintaining a viable relationship with the living God. Here are a few points that I have found helpful about prayer:

Christ is our mediator, and we pray in His name.

"You did not choose Me, but I chose you, and appointed you, that you would go and bear fruit, and that your fruit would remain, so that whatever you ask of the Father in My name, He may give to you" (John 15:16).

God is delighted when we pray.
"The sacrifice of the wicked is an abomination to the Lord, but the prayer of the upright is His delight" (Proverbs 15:8).

God hears and answers.
"LORD, thou hast heard the desire of the humble: thou wilt prepare their heart, thou wilt cause thine ear to hear" (Psalm 10:17, KJV).

"They called upon the LORD, and He answered them" (Psalm 99:6).

"Then you will call, and the LORD will answer; You will cry, and He will say, 'Here I am'" (Isaiah 58:9).

God's answers aren't always the same as our requests.
According to John 11, Martha and Mary wanted Jesus to heal Lazarus. He didn't. Instead, Jesus raised Lazarus from the dead to demonstrate the glory of God and to teach them regarding Himself when He said, "I am the resurrection and the life; he who believes in Me will live even if he dies" (John 11:25).

The apostle Paul prayed for his thorn in the flesh, apparently some physical ailment, to be removed, but God's answer was not to remove the thorn but rather to give Paul the grace to endure it (see 2 Corinthians 12:8-9).

Have you ever acquired God's grace for an impossible situation?

Sometimes God's answer is delayed, and sometimes His answer exceeds your request. Remember when the disciples prayed for imprisoned Peter? They couldn't believe it when he was actually released and knocked on the door of the house where they had gathered to pray (see Acts 12:1-16).

Can you think of a time when God answered over and above your expectations?

In Your Life

Any quality relationship involves good communication—both speaking and listening. If a teenager stops communicating, a family crisis is likely to result. The same can happen to us as spiritual children. Just like as building an earthly relationship requires time and attention, so our time alone with God is essential if our relationship with Him is to be open and comfortable.

Perhaps these ideas from Mable's handwritten folder "Time Alone with God" will help you as they have helped many others:

- Establish a time and a place for your meeting with God. Treat it like an appointment with a VIP, and if for some reason you cannot make it, set an alternative time. The deliberate time and place prepares you psychologically for the appointment.

- Believe that God is with you, even if you don't feel He is. Remember that God loves you and He wants to guide you toward meaning and purpose in your life, regardless of your current situation.

- Open your Bible and begin preparing your heart. Relax, be completely open and honest, and realize that God has X-ray eyes and ears. Begin with words like, "Lord, cleanse my heart so You can speak to me. Open my mind and alert my soul. Surround me with Your presence during this time and make me oblivious to everything else."

- Begin reading Scripture and think of it as God communicating with you while you listen. Pray the Scripture for you or for someone else. Mark or underline verses that jump out at you. In the margin of your Bible or in a notebook, write what you feel the Lord is telling you through the verses.

- Meditate about it, write it on a card, memorize it, and personalize it.

- If you are new to praying, you might find that the speaking time could be divided into a balance of A C T S:

Adoration or praise—Telling God that you love Him and why.

Confession—Cleansing your heart by agreeing with God about your sin.

Thanksgiving—Remembering all God has done for you. Bitterness and anger toward God and others cannot flourish in a thankful heart.

Supplication (requests, desires, definite needs)—Praying specific prayers will result in specific answers. This also includes intercession for others.

- Open up to God. As you learn to share your feelings, reactions, and attitudes with God, He will help you open up and improve your other relationships as well.
- Keep a small notebook to remind yourself of dates of prayers, prayers prayed for whom, and answers. Include a "Faith in Action" section. God may be leading you to become part of the answer. Pray in faith, believing that God hears and answers your prayers.
- Find a prayer partner or join a small prayer group.

Having our hearts tuned to Him is more relevant than the clock time. While many choose to pray in the mornings, Daniel, an Old Testament prophet, prayed three times a day (see Daniel 6:10). The psalmist, David, prayed at evening, in the morning, and at noon (see Psalm 55:17). Jesus prayed often—sometimes in the early morning (see Mark 1:35) or in the evening (see Matthew 14:23). From their examples we learn that regardless of the time of day set aside, prayer nurtures faith.

We can also infuse our lives with prayer by praying while walking, driving, waiting, or even praying with a friend over the phone. If we are committed and accountable, we will maintain our time with Him, not out of a sense of duty but because, like Mable, we love Him and want to know Him more. As the sports gear commercial says, "Just do it."

CHAPTER FIVE

Beyond Broken Dreams

Vernice Warden

My husband, Ray, and I were a typical young couple in the 1960s, rearing a son and daughter while working hard to maintain a family-run business. We made our share of mistakes, but we loved the Lord, were growing spiritually, and attended church regularly.

When our son, David, was nine years old, he accepted Christ as Savior, and two days later our seven-year-old daughter, Terri, also became a believer. As parents, Ray and I relied heavily on Proverbs 22:6: "Train up a child in the way he should go, even when he is old he will not depart from it."

After finishing college, David worked as a travel agent in Houston. Ray and I often discussed the sadness we felt each time we visited him. We couldn't pinpoint the problem, but our tall, handsome thirty-one-year-old son seemed lonely and miserable. For some reason he wasn't looking well.

One day after watching a television program describing AIDS, I couldn't help but wonder if David had the disease. Then I reprimanded myself for fretting and thinking our son might be caught up in a homosexual lifestyle. Still, nagging doubts remained.

A few weeks later, Ray tried contacting David and learned that he was in the hospital with pneumonia. Within thirty minutes, Ray and I were driving to Houston from our home near Dallas. When we arrived, David's weakened appearance frightened us both. At the motel that night, uncertainty kept me awake. Repeatedly I prayed, "O God, I need to know what's wrong. With your help I can handle it if someone will just tell me."

Early the next morning we drove to the hospital and waited in the hallway for David's return from the X-ray department. When a male nurse approached, I asked, "Is something else wrong with David besides pneumonia?"

The nurse looked at me and said, "You'll have to talk with his doctor." But the nurse's expression revealed the answer.

"I think I can tell you what's wrong," I said.

The nurse replied, "Tell me."

"I think David has AIDS."

The nurse's nod confirmed my greatest fears. Somehow God's grace strengthened me to receive the news, but AIDS seemed too impossible for Ray. He was overwhelmed and speechless.

David appeared frail and tired as attendants wheeled him back to his room. Because he'd been perspiring with a high fever, I asked, "David, would you let me wash your hair?"

"Sure," he said, managing a slight smile.

As I shampooed his brown hair we engaged in small talk, and I inwardly prayed, *Lord, give me the courage to say what I need to say.*

After David's hair was dry and combed, I looked at him and said gently, "David . . . Son . . . we know you have AIDS."

His brown eyes registered both surprise and hurt. Finally, I couldn't hold back the tears. Ray put his arm around me and I reached for David. The three of us held each other and wept for a long time.

Between sobs, David whispered, "I love you."

I promised David, "We'll get through this . . . somehow." Together our family began a new course in our lives, a journey we never expected.

The doctor told us David could live from six months to two years. At that time, in 1985, we didn't want anyone to know about David's disease. We hoped an AIDS cure would be found, David would recover, and everything could somehow return to normal.

Later, a part of me cried, *How could he do this to us? We'd provided a Christian home. AIDS happened in other families, not ours.* Privately and tearfully, Ray and I discussed our anger, hurt, and embarrassment. We believed homosexuality was included among the sins against God given in Romans 1:18-32, and we didn't approve of our son's lifestyle. But how could we abandon him when he needed us most? We didn't understand what had happened to David, but we chose to forgive him and extend unconditional love. Time shouted, "David is dying."

So we offered David the option of moving closer to home, even moving in with us if necessary. After his release from the hospital, he moved within thirty miles, living and working in Dallas for a year. But during the second year, his damaged immune system gave rise to shingles and the cytomegalovirus that invaded his eyes, leaving him legally blind. When he could no longer drive or live alone, we brought him into our home.

AIDS was destroying the nerve centers in David's brain, causing seizures and disorientation. He could no longer think clearly and rationally. We never knew what to expect. Sometimes he was affectionate, but other times he exploded with fits of anger. Each morning we boarded an emotional roller coaster.

How could we cope? Could we continue caring for David? Were we doing the right thing? Questions whirled through my mind. After all, Ray and I were enjoying freedom to travel and grandparenting Terri and her husband's children, a stage of life we'd joyfully anticipated. Adjusting to home care of our son and his debilitating disease was not easy.

But God provided the strength I needed to cook nutritious meals and do the extra cleaning necessary. Ray was supportive and helpful. Terri visited often, bringing her refreshing sense of humor like a splash of cool water on a hot day. With their help and my meditating on Scripture, especially the Psalms—"He alone is my rock and my salvation; he is my fortress, I will not be shaken" (Psalm 62:6, NIV)—I made it through, step by step.

While the physical demands stretched me to the limit, the emotional and spiritual traumas were too much to handle alone. Finally, I sought the help of a Christian counselor. She helped me identify false guilt and said that Ray and I were watching the results of David's life choices. Still, I kept remembering Proverbs 22:6. *Did God fail us?*

From Dr. John White's book *Parents in Pain*,[1] I learned that Proverbs is a collection of inspired observations by wise and godly men. It includes examples of both good and bad parents, of both good and disobedient children. The best training cannot instill wisdom, but only encourages the choice to seek it. If God's created son, Adam, chose the folly of disobedience, then how can the wisest parents on earth guarantee wisdom or godliness in their children? These insights helped release me from the haunting feelings of failure.

My counselor helped me realize that by taking on the guilt and responsibility for David's actions, I was, in a way, exercising a controlling and independent attitude. In doing so, I was leaving God completely out! As my counselor said, I could not be solely responsible—I couldn't be that powerful.

As David's health worsened, we divulged the truth to our families, our pastor, our friend who was the funeral home director, and a couple of neighbors. Each reacted differently, but all were kind. By that time, our emotions were so fragile we couldn't have handled rejection.

Our pastor visited David often and nurtured an amiable relationship. He sat near David's bed and held his hand as they discussed many things, including heaven.

Young, creative, intelligent David eventually relinquished hope of living on earth and realized his only hope was in Christ alone. We believed without a doubt—and our pastor reassured us—that David had made his peace with God. With my help, David memorized Scriptures that he recited during his last days, including

"When I am afraid, I will put my trust in You" (Psalm 56:3). David repeatedly thanked us for not deserting him.

As his condition became critical in May of 1988, I knew our skeleton-like son was ready to go — and we had to let him. Seeing his deterioration was heartbreaking. I dreaded the finality of death, but longed for his suffering to end.

One day Terri came. When David began lapsing in and out of consciousness, I phoned his doctor for reassurance one last time. A short time later, as we tenderly wiped his arms and forehead and told him we loved him, David took his last breath. Terri turned to me and cried, "We did it, Mother! I didn't know if we could take care of David until the end, but we did it!" As we hugged and sobbed, I felt hurt, exhausted, relieved, and empty, but also inexplicably at peace.

Throughout the ordeal, I remembered Christ's response to sinners. He always treated them with dignity and respect. I couldn't be responsible for David's choices, but I was responsible for mine. Although my faith had often been weak and wavering, I reached the point that I didn't have to know all the reasons why — I just knew God could handle any problem. I felt His comfort as I grieved David's death and its cause.

Before David's illness I tended to be judgmental of others, but taking care of our son taught me more about forgiveness and compassion. Now when I encounter other parents facing a child with AIDS, I reach out with empathy, encouraging them with my testimony of God's faithfulness and my understanding of the disease. Just as Christ is patient and forgiving toward me, I can treat others the same. Yes, David required sacrificial love, but I'll never regret giving it. Most of all, I learned the true meaning of 2 Corinthians 12:9: "My grace is sufficient for thee" (KJV).

Faithlifter
Forgiveness

IN HER SHOES

Vernice's account provides a living illustration of how a family pulled together during a crisis, each contributing selflessly for the good of all. Had they responded in a judgmental, unforgiving way toward David, this story would have ended rather differently. David made some poor decisions, but his parents chose to forgive him and love him through it all. Isn't that what Christ does for us?

C. S. Lewis has stated, "Everyone says forgiveness is a lovely idea until he has something to forgive."[2] Forgiveness is not easy, but to grow in faith, we must take the first step. Just as it is possible to change, it is possible to forgive.

Has forgiving someone been a challenge for you? How was God's grace evident in the lives of this family?

IN HIS WORD

The Bible has a great deal to say about forgiveness. Here are a few points I have found helpful:

Forgiveness doesn't start with us. It begins with God.

This is expressed clearly in Scripture. "If we confess our sins, He is faithful and righteous to forgive us our sins and to cleanse us from all unrighteousness" (1 John 1:9).

Mart DeHaan states, "The Bible says that the story of forgiveness begins with God. He once and for all forgives the past, present, and future sins of all who accept the cross of His Son as payment for our moral debts. He purges our record in the courts of heaven and secures forever the legal acquittal of all who trust His Son."[3]

We are to extend grace in the matter of forgiveness.
DeHaan continues: "With such immeasurable forgiveness in view, Jesus tells the story of a man who was forgiven of a multimillion-dollar debt, but who turned around and refused to forgive the debt of one who owed him a relatively small amount of money (Matthew 18:21-35). Our Teacher used the story to show how immoral it is for us to take mountains of mercy from Him, and then to turn around and withhold a few shovels of that mercy from those who ask us."[4]

Just as we have received God's forgiveness, we are commanded to let the attitude of forgiveness overflow into the lives of others. Jesus said, "Be on your guard! If your brother sins, rebuke him; and if he repents, forgive him. And if he sins against you seven times a day, and returns to you seven times, saying, 'I repent,' forgive him" (Luke 17:3-4).

Receive God's grace and do not let bitterness grow.

It requires God's grace to forgive, especially in painful situations, but His grace is sufficient if we allow Him to work in our hearts. We are warned of the danger of failing to receive His grace. "See to it that no one comes short of the grace of God; that no root of bitterness springing up causes trouble, and by it many be defiled" (Hebrews 12:15). And the apostle Paul wrote, "Be kind to one another, tender-hearted, forgiving each other, just as God in Christ also has forgiven you" (Ephesians 4:32).

IN YOUR LIFE
Forgiving others is one of the most difficult challenges of life, especially when we have been deeply hurt. But trusting God in this matter is crucial to our spiritual health. James Coulter has written, "The unforgiving spirit as a pride form is the number one killer of spiritual life."[5]

Perhaps these insights will offer some practical help:

Let the pot drop.
Don Anderson, author and family counselor, wrote: "In the New Testament, the word translated forgiveness has several meanings. My

favorite is 'Let the pot drop.' Don't you love it? Can't you see this person walking around carrying all of his resentments in this big pot and now he is instructed to drop it. Wow! What a relief."[6]

Forgiveness is not just a one-time proposition but rather an attitude of heart, a way of life. Because of stubbornness, arrogance, hard-heartedness, and pride, we sometimes fail to love as Christ loved. Instead of hoarding or cherishing offenses, we can let them go. Let the pot drop!

Hold others accountable.

Mart DeHaan also addresses accountability. He suggests that if someone offends us, we can go to that person and speak the truth in love. The relationship will suffer if the offense is simply "swept under the rug" and forgiven unconditionally. It is a sign of honor to hold people accountable for their actions, and if we simply rationalize hurts or deny them, we allow selfish or bad behavior to continue and the relationship to remain strained. A more open and honest relationship will result from confrontation, forgiveness, and resolution.

We may consider a simple question such as "Do you realize how that made me feel?" or "I love you too much to ignore what you did." Sometimes a stronger rebuke is needed, but the idea is to build up rather than to tear down (see Ephesians 4:29). This approach works best when a good relationship has already been established.[7]

Forgiveness does not eliminate consequences.

We may forgive, but the consequences of the offense remain. God forgave Adam and Eve, but He banished them from the garden. God forgave David for adultery with Bathsheba, but the child born of that union died when just seven days old. The Wardens forgave their son, but he still died of AIDS. We may forgive a family member of abuse, but the scars remain. God does not suspend His law of "sowing and reaping" (see Galatians 6:7-8). In forgiveness He removes the eternal guilt but not all of the resulting consequences of our sin.

Remember that God is sovereign.

Consider the biblical example of Joseph, who endured some of life's toughest circumstances. Few illustrations of forgiveness are more touching than when he spoke to his brothers: "You intended to harm me, but God intended it for good to accomplish what is now being done, the saving of many lives" (Genesis 50:20, NIV).

Pray for your offender.

Resentment fades in the prayer closet as we become more aware of our offender's humanity and his needs. Perhaps through the process of forgiveness God wants you to learn an advanced lesson in servanthood. If you remain teachable, none of your experiences will be wasted. I've found that true in my life.

Lewis Smedes wrote this word picture:

> When you forgive someone for hurting you, you perform spiritual surgery inside your soul; you cut away the wrong that was done to you. . . . Detach that person from the hurt and let it go, the way a child opens his hands and lets a trapped butterfly go free.
>
> Then invite that person back into your mind, fresh, as if a piece of history between you had been rewritten, its grip on your memory broken. Reverse the seemingly irreversible flow of pain within you.[8]

CHAPTER SIX

Compassion Is the Key

Cherry Brown

As a full-time homemaker and the mother of two teenagers, I felt the winds of change blowing through my soul. It seemed the Lord was preparing me for something new, but I didn't know what.

One morning after my husband, Charles, had left for work and Chuck and Rhonda were off to school, I opened the Bible to begin my morning quiet time. Almost immediately I felt a prompting in a direction I never had imagined. It seemed the Lord spoke to my heart and said, "Cherry, Greenville needs a Christian bookstore."

I thought about the many people who could use Bibles and Christian literature. I envisioned mothers, dads, and children who needed to know God's love and to experience His love in their homes. A Christian bookstore would be a great ministry for people in my community who longed for the stability only His Word could provide. As Isaiah 40:8 says, "The grass withers, the flower fades, but the word of our God stands forever."

At that point in my life, I had never set foot in a Christian bookstore, having purchased most of my books through the mail. But the more I thought about it, the more excited I became. Right away I formulated a list of people who might provide information to help me get started.

That evening, I told Charles and our teens about my brainstorm. They loved the idea! Charles had set aside some money from his construction business, and he readily offered financial and emotional support. Our family prayed together, "Lord, if You are in this, open the door."

The door flew open the following week when I found economical rental space. After several inquiries and telephone calls, I located a small discounted space in a shopping center for fifty dollars a month. The owner told me, "I was just thinking it would be nice to have a Christian bookstore in the area." That seemed to be further confirmation as I thought, *If I can't pay fifty dollars a month for rent, this certainly must not be God's will.*

Then a friend and former church secretary familiar with the publishing industry helped me locate names and addresses of different publishers. I visited Virginia's Christian Bookstore in Dallas because I had heard that Virginia, a seasoned owner, cared about her customers and screened her books for doctrinal soundness. Her store had a reputation for carrying excellent Bibles, books, and materials, so when she invited me to peruse her shelves, I took notes and asked lots of questions.

Later I met with a representative who gave me a stern lecture about how hard it was to make a living in the business. If I had doubted God's will, I would have quit right then. Still, I felt God's leading, and He brought others into my life who helped me gain a balanced perspective. But getting started was not easy. It took about two months from the time we began researching the subject until the opening. When the big day finally arrived, I put an ad in the local newspaper and kept Rhonda out of school so she could help with checking out all the customers I just knew would flock to Cherry's Christian Bookstore.

Guess what? Hardly anyone came to the "grand opening," and I sent Rhonda back to school at noon. Later that week, only one person came in, and my total sale for the day was $2.95. That really caused me to doubt my new business venture! But because I cared about people, I continued anyway, even though the income was small.

That plan paid off. The bookstore eventually began flourishing, and we moved into a larger location nearer the interstate highway, where the city was expanding. One day a young man came into the store selling cookware, and Mary, one of my employees, and I told him we didn't need any. He confided that because he had not made any sales that day, he couldn't afford to buy gasoline for his drive home to Dallas.

I told Mary to give him some money from the cash drawer while I handed him some tracts. He was so impressed and grateful that he asked what he could do to repay us.

"Go buy your gas," I said, "and then come back so we can share Jesus with you."

Prayerfully we waited, and to our surprise and delight he soon walked in and said, "I bought my gas. Now I'm ready to listen."

After I shared the plan of salvation, he bowed his head and prayed to receive Christ. Then he said, "Now I know why I came to Greenville today instead of going to Denton as I had planned."

Surely a divine appointment had occurred, and I shudder to think what might have happened if we had not given him money for gasoline.

Many times my servant-hearted employees would minister to people who came into the store. One lady who came from another town said, "We have a Christian bookstore in our community, but I always come here because you make me feel special." That was our goal. Like the Good Samaritan, I wanted each individual to feel valued and loved. Often my employees or I would take time to pray with someone who had a special need. I have no idea how many books, pamphlets, and cards I personally gave away. If I could lift someone's heavy burden or coax a smile from young or old, my day had been worthwhile.

One time when I locked the store after a long day, I juggled my keys, briefcase, purse, and bottled water before hearing an unfamiliar voice growl, "Lady, I need all your money!" I laughed, thinking the man was joking. When he repeated his command, I turned, looked at him compassionately, and countered with my soft southern accent, "Sir, won't you please let me tell you about Jesus?"

"No, lady," the thief barked, "give me your money!"

Holding the day's cash in my briefcase, I calmly opened my purse and pulled out eighty dollars. My heart pounded as the nervous man grabbed it and left. That was only one example of the many adventures I encountered day after day. At times I felt the Lord's protection shielding me while I shared His love with others.

Colossians 3:23 was always a motivation to me: "Whatever you do, do your work heartily, as for the Lord rather than for men." I did not draw a salary for the first two years but just continued to invest in the business. However, I didn't worry because the eternal investments always exceeded monetary value.

After twenty-two years, Charles and I felt it was time to sell the store and spend more time with each other and our family. Just prior to the new owners coming, Charles placed a decorative rural mailbox on a table so people could express their thoughts about the store and what it had meant to them through the years. Many loyal customers wrote letters and placed them inside the box. Now as I read through their notes, I experience a collage of both laughter and tears.

These are a few excerpts:

"Cherry, when I was a new Christian moving into the community, you were the first friendly person I encountered. Thank you for allowing the love of Jesus to flow through you."

"I will miss the lovely graciousness of your store. Thank you for always caring for me and for my family."

"Thank you, Cherry, that you always called me by name."

"It was always so good to see your smiling face."

"Thank you for encouraging my children and for providing spiritual guidance through your materials."

"Thank you for taking time to talk and cry with me when I was at a low ebb. God used you to comfort me and encourage me through His Word."

It was difficult to leave the store, but I always knew that when we serve others, we are really serving our Lord.

Faithlifter
Compassion

IN HER SHOES

Someone wisely said that people will not care what you know until they know that you care. Compassion is that quality that causes a person to identify with someone else's need. It is truly like walking in another's shoes and putting yourself in that place. Cherry demonstrated compassion for people in her community by obeying the vision to provide Bibles and Christian literature that would help strengthen their faith and enable them to navigate the storms in their lives.

Cherry's caring response to the thief indicates she was more interested in his soul than in her own personal safety. She went above and beyond her duty in reaching out to others by investing a great deal of time and energy in her bookstore. Why were people so responsive to Cherry? What lessons can we learn from her experiences?

IN HIS WORD

Compassion is one of the attributes of God that we may study and apply to our lives today. "The LORD is gracious and righteous; our God is full of compassion" (Psalm 116:5, NIV). "So, as those who have been chosen of God, holy and beloved, put on a heart of compassion, kindness, humility, gentleness and patience" (Colossians 3:12).

Compassion can be explained as sympathy or sorrow over the misfortune of others. "God told Moses, '*I'm* in charge of mercy. *I'm* in charge of compassion.' Compassion doesn't originate in our bleeding hearts or moral sweat, but in God's mercy" (Romans 9:15, MSG).

The Greek word *sumpatheo* describes Christ's sympathy and suffering with others. Its meaning is expanded in Hebrews 4:15: "For we do not have a high priest who is unable to sympathize with our weaknesses, but we have one who has been tempted in every way, just as we are—yet was without sin" (NIV). In short, Jesus hurts when we hurt. Here are a few examples of Christ's compassion:

Jesus cared for physical needs.

"And Jesus called His disciples to Him, and said, 'I feel compassion for the people, because they have remained with Me now three days and have nothing to eat; and I do not want to send them away hungry, for they might faint on the way'" (Matthew 15:32).

He healed the blind. "They said to Him, 'Lord, we want our eyes to be opened.' Moved with compassion, Jesus touched their eyes; and immediately they regained their sight and followed Him" (Matthew 20:33-34).

Jesus cared for emotional needs.

"And when the Lord saw her, He felt compassion for her, and said to her, 'Do not weep'" (Luke 7:13).

"For he will deliver the needy when he cries for help, the afflicted also, and him who has no helper. He will have compassion on the poor and needy, and the lives of the needy he will save" (Psalm 72:12-13).

Jesus cared for spiritual needs.

"The Lord is not slow about His promise, as some count slowness, but is patient toward you, not wishing for any to perish but for all to come to repentance" (2 Peter 3:9).

Of course, Jesus' greatest demonstration of compassion was when He took our sins upon Himself and sacrificed His very life for us on the cross. That is the ultimate in compassion.

"The LORD's lovingkindnesses indeed never cease, for His compassions never fail. They are new every morning; great is Your faithfulness" (Lamentations 3:22-23).

IN YOUR LIFE

Just as we have received God's compassion, we can open our hearts and share it with others. Compassion may come more naturally to some people than others. Perhaps these suggestions will help:

Pray for compassion.

Scripture says, "Love the Lord your God with all your passion and prayer and muscle and intelligence—and . . . love your neighbor as well as you do yourself" (Luke 10:27, MSG). Loving your neighbor is sometimes more difficult than loving God, but that's where your faith is stretched. Ask God's Spirit to help you.

Practice compassion.

Start with your family. Compassion begins at home. I once knew a lady who worked feverishly feeding the homeless at a shelter while her starving family back home had to fend for themselves. Compassion begins in our families and then extends into the highways and byways of life.

Teach your children to show compassion.

A recent news article referred to many of today's youth as "the new barbarians"—self-centered, self-seeking young men and women who have never been taught compassion. As parents and grandparents, you can make a difference by teaching your sons and daughters what it means to really care about others. Take them to visit elderly, homebound friends; take them along to deliver food or flowers to a grieving family or to welcome a new baby; as a family, buy Christmas gifts for the needy and deliver them.

Use your imagination and make plans according to your circumstances and the ages of your children. We teach compassion to our children and youth by the way we treat them and by how they observe us treat others.

Let your body language show that you care.

Simply facing a person, making eye contact, or moving closer while conversing demonstrates your interest. Some people require more physical space and do not wish to be hugged or touched—and we should respect that. But as a nurse, I've found that most patients appreciate an extended hand or touch on the shoulder. Looking into their eyes and listening with the heart conveys your sensitivity. Some people with the gift of mercy find such expressions come easily, but that doesn't excuse the rest of us from finding ways to express the caring attitude of Christ.

Make a telephone call or write a note to lift a hurting soul.

Have you ever had a "down day," only to be refreshed by a telephone call or a note from a friend? The Lord knows who needs special attention, and when you feel a prompting to pray for or contact someone, you should heed that prompting. By following through, you show your compassion.

Put yourself in her shoes.

When I have difficulty relating to someone, I think about how I would feel if I were in her situation and how I would wish to be treated.

Ken Gire wrote: "Before we can love our neighbor, we must see our neighbor and hear our neighbor. Observing the way a gardener observes plants. Watching their buds when they're blooming. Watering their roots when they're wilting. But we cannot weep with those who weep or rejoice with those who rejoice unless we first see something of their tears or hear something of their laughter. If we can learn to see and hear our neighbor, maybe, just maybe, we can learn to see and hear God. And seeing Him and hearing Him, to love Him. To passionately love God and other people. This is what matters. This is all that matters. And all that God requires. But it requires our all to fulfill."[1]

CHAPTER SEVEN

When Suicide Hits Home

Fran Caffey Sandin

Clouds hid the January sun; an eerie fog blanketed the earth. From my cozy kitchen table I could imagine the chill outside as I read a morning devotional and planned the week's agenda. The ringing phone shattered my reverie.

"Hello," I answered cheerfully.

A solemn voice responded, "Fran?"

I recognized the voice of a neighbor and longtime friend of my parents. Her voice was low and steady. "Fran, this is Ruth. Your mother needs you right away. Come immediately and bring Jim."

"What happened?" I gasped.

"Just come as quickly as you can. Just come," Ruth finished with a whisper.

I responded, "We'll be there as soon as possible."

The urgency and secrecy of Ruth's message struck me as I hung up and dialed my husband's office. Ordinarily on a Monday Jim would have been performing surgery at the hospital. But he was working at the office instead.

"Don't worry," his secretary responded. "We'll take care of rescheduling patients. I'll give Dr. Sandin your message."

As soon as Jim arrived, we started the one-hour drive to my family's home. We knew that something drastic had occurred. But what?

My seventy-one-year-old dad had been struggling with depression and for several months had experienced insomnia and weight loss. His family doctor, who had successfully treated Dad for depression a few years earlier, had started him on a similar treatment that included a mild sleeping pill and antidepressant medication.

As a nurse, I was curious about the medications. When I researched information on both of them, one paragraph included a warning: "Use with caution in patients with suicidal tendencies." I had skimmed over those words, thinking, *That doesn't pertain to Dad.* The medications seemed suitable for his age and his problem. Now the caution brought a sickening feeling. Still, I thought, *Not my dad.*

Everyone who knew Dad recognized him as a solid citizen. He was conscientious, dependable, honorable, encouraging to others, and a stabilizing force in our family. His love for the Lord was evidenced by years of unselfish service to his church and community. I was proud of Dad. I knew he wasn't perfect, but to me he seemed invincible.

The knowledge of Dad's depression made us uneasy as we traveled, but Jim and I were hoping that Mother only needed some assistance in making an important decision regarding his care. When we arrived, my heart skipped a beat. A police car and an ambulance were parked in the driveway.

"It can't be," I whispered.

Jim and I entered the house quickly, only to hear my mother cry, "I just can't believe it. He shot himself!"

I couldn't believe what I heard. How could he have done this? It was so out-of-character for my gentle father. None of us had realized the depth of his distress, not even Mother. *Couldn't we have done something to help him?*

I recalled the previous Wednesday when my sister and I had

visited in their home. For the first time I could remember, Dad revealed some of his deepest feelings.

"I feel worthless," he said, nervously rubbing his hands together. "I'm having trouble concentrating. I read too slowly."

"But Dad," I interrupted, "you are not worthless. You are precious to God and to your family. We all love you. Since you retired, you may feel you're not useful, but you are. You are important whether or not you do anything, but you will feel better about yourself if you accomplish something each day."

He nodded as I continued. "Can you think of any of your neighbors who needs a visit? Let's make a list of a few things you can do each day. As you achieve a goal, mark it off the list. Then you'll feel better about yourself."

"Several people I know could use a visit," he responded, "and I could probably help Gaston clear some land."

"That sounds great," I said. Together we designed a plan of action.

"Do you have some comfortable shoes?" I asked. "Maybe you and Mother could take a walk every day. The exercise would be refreshing."

During our conversation, I tried to encourage Dad by sharing some favorite verses. Then I thought of something. "I don't think I've ever asked you before, but would you tell us how you came to know Christ as your Savior?"

Without hesitation, he related his experience. "You know Daddy and Mama always took us to church, and when I was about eight years old, one of my Sunday school teachers took a special interest in me. When she shared the plan of salvation, I understood it. During the altar call that day, I walked down the church aisle to publicly confess Jesus as my Savior. I knew the Holy Spirit came into my heart."

Then he added, "The last few nights when I couldn't sleep, I've meditated on Psalm 23."

Before leaving, I prayed with Dad. In the doorway I stopped, gave him a hug, and warmly added, "I love you, Dad." Those were my last words to him.

Saturday I had called Mother. "Your dad seems better," she reported. "We've been walking, and he has been following his plan. I believe he is making progress."

"Tell Dad I love him and I'll see him on Wednesday," I said, feeling somewhat relieved.

But now as I reflected on our visit, I wondered, *Did I sound arrogant or preachy? Was I so busy trying to fix Dad that I failed to listen? Was I oblivious to his need for more medical help?*

It never occurred to me that Dad might be considering suicide. Or had he acted impulsively that Monday morning when he first awoke? Now, as I recalled our parting, guilt took hold of my conscience. *You call yourself a nurse,* it seemed to scold. *Why didn't you see the signs? He was dropping hints, but you were blind and deaf. Shame on you!*

Inwardly I crumbled. Suicide is a double blow. Not only do we grieve the death, but we also grieve the cause of death. For a time I felt overwhelmed. It seemed the *if-only* and *why-didn't-I* questions would never cease.

About a week after Dad's memorial service, anger began to take hold. I was angry at Dad for leaving us and angry at us for not stopping him. It took months for me to work through the maze of turmoil and confusion.

For a time, I struggled spiritually. "God, where are You?" I cried. "Why did You let this happen?"

I was no stranger to grief. In 1974 our seventeen-month-old son, Jeffrey—the youngest of our three children—died of bacterial meningitis. But this time the grief I felt seemed different.

Though I knew intellectually that God was with me, He seemed far away. I longed to feel His presence, but for weeks I felt forsaken. Had God pulled down the shade? My emptiness and loneliness made me doubt my sanity. Finally I decided to visit a Christian counselor to talk through my concerns. I told him, "I need someone who doesn't know me to objectively say, 'You're okay.'"

After hearing my story, the counselor reassured me that my response was normal following a loved one's suicide. He encouraged me, "With time, friends, and prayer, I think you will be able to handle the painful death of your father."

My counselor was right.

Eventually I realized that Dad was ill. Just as some people have physical illnesses, others have mental and emotional sicknesses. Dad did not want to burden anyone, even his family, with his problems. Yet behind the smile on his face had been a man with a troubled spirit.

The question "Why?" will remain, but a few clues were apparent. First, Dad's melancholy temperament often dominated his life, causing him to see negatives instead of positives in himself.

Also, years of cigarette smoking had replaced his youthful appearance and his wonderful singing voice with emphysema. A year before his suicide he finally had been able to give up smoking. But the counselor told me, "Nicotine withdrawal could have contributed to the depth of your father's depression."

Further, Dad resisted assistance. A man from Dad's generation expected to be able to handle everything. To ask for help was not masculine. For several months before his death, Dad suspected something was wrong with his reasoning skills, but he seemed fine when he was around others. He told Mother, "I do not want to see a psychiatrist. I'm worried about what my Christian friends would think."

My brother, sister, and I honored Dad; we never considered making him do anything against his will. If we had intervened and forced him to be hospitalized, would the outcome have been different? Only the Lord knows.

More than likely, Dad was not choosing death as much as he was trying to end unbearable emotional anguish. Complex issues were involved. Dad felt unable to cope.

How does a Christian daughter come to terms with the suicide of her father? Not easily. But during the healing process I've learned once again the importance of having a personal relationship with Jesus Christ.

Dad's suicide was devastating, but I'm glad he knew the Savior. According to Scripture, I believe Dad is with Him now (see John 6:37; 10:28-29).

I am a sinner, too. I know that I disappoint God with my stubborn reluctance to admit it at times. But just as a parent loves a child in spite of his disobedience, God loves us when we belong to Him through Christ. God forgives our sin not because we deserve it, but because of His grace.

If the blood of Christ is powerful enough to cover my sin, it covers my father's sin, too. Because Christ forgives me, I can forgive my father. I can also stop blaming myself for his death.

Guilt followed me until one day at a friend's home I saw a card that read, "I refuse to accept responsibility for that which I cannot control." Then it dawned on me: I could not be responsible for Dad's final decision. Part of my anger resulted from being unable to control what had happened. Now it was time to let go of my guilt, forgive myself, and realize that some secrets are locked up until eternity (see Deuteronomy 29:29).

I am also reminded that life is precious. Each one is created in God's image with a unique contribution and influence. I remember how much Dad enjoyed music, and I think of him as I play the organ. When I sing our national anthem and see the flag, I get a lump in my throat, remembering Dad's patriotism and service to his country in World War II. Family photographs remind me of his role as a caring granddad. We loved him. We miss him.

I have been comforted by these words: "For I am convinced that neither death nor life, neither angels nor demons, neither the present nor the future, nor any powers, neither height nor depth, nor anything else in all creation, will be able to separate us from the love of God that is in Christ Jesus our Lord" (Romans 8:38-39, NIV).

Grief recovery is a slow process, but now I know the Lord did not forsake me. Our friends' prayers and gifts were tangible expressions of His love. The peace He has placed in my heart reminds me that nothing is beyond His reach. Christ can heal any pain.

Faithlifter
Hope

In Her Shoes

I wrote this very painful personal story to help others who might be facing similar circumstances. It seemed my dad had come to the end of his physical, mental, and emotional resources, but for reasons I do not understand, he was unable to appropriate the supernatural grace of God for his need. Perhaps an evil spirit tormented him, or his physical problems demanded more attention than we realized. We don't know. I think Dad arrived in heaven a little earlier than God would have desired, but that does not change God's love for him, nor mine.

Have you ever experienced a night of the soul in which hope did not exist apart from God? Did you sense His stability and strength during that time? Did you feel angry toward Him? Were you able to rest in Him instead of demanding answers?

In His Word

While the word *hope* in our modern lingo has come to mean something we wish would happen — "I hope we win the game," "I hope it rains" — in the Bible, *hope* means "assurance."

In the New Testament, the Greek word for *hope* means "favorable and confident expectation." It describes the happy anticipation of good: "in the hope of eternal life, which God, who cannot lie, promised long ages ago" (Titus 1:2).

A close connection exists between joy and hope. "Now may the God of hope fill you with all joy and peace in believing, so that you will abound in hope by the power of the Holy Spirit" (Romans 15:13).

The basis for hope is seen in these verses: ". . . to whom God willed to make known what is the riches of the glory of this mystery among the Gentiles, which is Christ in you, the hope of glory" (Colossians 1:27) and "Paul, an apostle of Christ Jesus according to the commandment of God our Savior, and of Christ Jesus, who is our hope" (1 Timothy 1:1).

Hope is described as "good": "Now may our Lord Jesus Christ Himself and God our Father, who has loved us and given us eternal comfort and good hope by grace, comfort and strengthen your hearts in every good work and word" (2 Thessalonians 2:16-17).

Hope is blessed: ". . . looking for the blessed hope and the appearing of the glory of our great God and Savior, Christ Jesus" (Titus 2:13).

Hope is living: "Blessed be the God and Father of our Lord Jesus Christ, who according to His great mercy has caused us to be born again to a living hope through the resurrection of Jesus Christ from the dead" (1 Peter 1:3).

IN YOUR LIFE

If we place our hope in people or in things—our careers, the economy, our spouses, our children, our possessions—we will be disappointed. Hope based on mankind's plan is shaky because the foundation is not firm. However, since God is the author of hope, we can trust in His promises.

Hope in God alone.

Lisa Beamer, whose husband, Todd, led the attack against the hijackers of United Flight 93 on September 11, 2001, explained how she felt after watching the television news that morning. Before receiving the official call regarding Todd's death, she knew in her heart that he had died in that plane crash.

"For days I would struggle to deal with the shock," she said. "And yet, in that dark moment of my soul, I first cried out to God. I knew without a doubt that my hope wasn't based on Todd or any other human being. Nor was it based even on life itself, when I got right down to it. My faith wasn't rooted in governments, religion, tall buildings, or frail people. Instead, my faith and my security were in God."[1]

Don't be a "lone ranger."

My pastor once quipped that even the Lone Ranger had Tonto! One of the functions of the body of believers is to foster encouragement, love, and hope. When a believer chooses isolation, Satan often attacks him as a lion grabs a lamb straying from the flock. The lion is unlikely to attack the entire flock, but the stray is easy prey (see 1 Peter 5:8). Our church fellowship reminds us to hope in Christ, regardless of our circumstances.

Look to the future.

The very word *hope* looks to the future, not the past. " 'For I know the plans that I have for you,' declares the LORD, 'plans for welfare and not for calamity to give you a future and a hope' " (Jeremiah 29:11). As you lock arms with God's promises, you are able to view life in a new light. Even the events that you would not choose can be woven together for good in God's scheme of things. Your disappointments can become divine appointments for something better you cannot see.

Look to the Resurrection.

Our hope is securely wrapped in the resurrection of Jesus Christ, who said, "I am the resurrection and the life; he who believes in Me shall live even if he dies, and everyone who lives and believes in Me shall never die. Do you believe this?" (John 11:25-26).

Believers can rest assured that faith, hope, and life walk hand in hand. Richard Sibbes wrote, "The nature of hope is to expect that which faith believes."[2]

CHAPTER EIGHT

The Rainbow Connection

Denise Davis

The carefree excitement of my first pregnancy gave way to grave concern after my seventh-month prenatal checkup in August of 1996. I had not felt the baby moving very much, and I expressed my uneasiness to the doctor.

"Well," he explained matter-of-factly, "as the fetus gets bigger, it sometimes doesn't move as much."

But after he attached a monitor and did a few non-stress tests, I could tell from his expression that he was not pleased. The baby was not as active as he should be, and at times his heart rate dropped.

"Denise," the doctor said thoughtfully, "I want you to come back tomorrow morning for more testing. We need to find out what's going on here."

My husband, Keith, a church music and youth director, pampered me at home. While resting, I thought about the day's happenings and wondered what to expect. I had called my parents with a report and asked them to pray.

The following morning as I waited alone after the tests were completed, the perinatologist entered my room and explained that the ultrasound confirmed our son, Skylar, had IUGR—intrauterine growth retardation. To my surprise he said, "It has probably been six weeks since the fetus has had adequate nutrition, so basically he has been starving in the womb."

"It's not too late to terminate this pregnancy. You can still abort the fetus," the doctor suggested with a positive tone. "The chances are very good that the fetus is severely mentally retarded, brain-damaged, handicapped, and seriously malformed. His legs are probably shorter than normal, and with his failure to thrive, we cannot predict what other problems you may encounter. He may even die at birth."

"Abortion?" I looked at the doctor with disbelief. "No, this is my baby!" I tried not to show the anger that welled up inside. *How dare he even suggest that I kill my baby!* For me, abortion was not an option.

About that time, Keith and our pastor walked in. With my voice quivering, I asked the doctor, "Would you please tell them what you just told me?"

When the doctor bluntly repeated the information, Keith's immediate response was firm. "Doctor, you are talking about 'the fetus.' That is not just a fetus; it is Skylar, our son. We want to have our baby and, even if he dies in our arms, we would rather have a few minutes holding him than to know that he died at our own hands, that we killed him." Our pastor nodded in approval.

After Keith spoke, the doctor's countenance softened as he turned to me and gave his instructions. "Then I need you to go to the hospital and begin steroid treatments now through Friday to strengthen the baby's lungs."

That never happened. About an hour after I arrived at the hospital, Skylar's heart rate plummeted, his distress became apparent, and the nurses called the doctor, who said, "We'll have to do an emergency C-section now."

We had recently moved to the Austin, Texas, area and had made a few friends, but no one as close as our own family. I tried to remain

cool and calm as I called Mom and said, "Well, come if you can."
But inside, my emotions churned like a steam engine as I thought,
Please come now, please come now, please come now! Mom and Dad
started the four-hour journey, but the doctor could not wait for
them, and surgery began with Keith at my side.

In a gentle manner the doctor asked, "Denise, do you want us
to tell you what he looks like before you see him? This baby could
be very deformed." He paused and then said, "Are you sure you want
to see him at all?"

"Yes, I want to see him!" Because I didn't know if he would survive, I didn't want to miss a chance to hold our baby.

During Skylar's birth, Keith remained strong and confident that
everything would be okay. As his eyes locked onto mine, I felt our
love growing in a new dimension.

When the doctor reached in to retrieve the baby, Skylar belted
out a cry that sounded like a bleating little lamb. Immediately Keith
and I began weeping because we felt the Lord's presence hovering
near, definitely impressing us that our baby would be okay. Skylar
came out with his eyes open, and at two pounds, five ounces, he was
perfectly formed, just very tiny. We got only a brief look at him and
a quick kiss before the attendant whisked him off to the neonatal
care unit.

In the meantime, Mom and Dad continued driving, easing their
apprehension by quoting Scriptures to one another and praying.
Texas summers are normally hot and dry, but a brief, unexpected
thunderstorm left a fine mist in the air. Then as the clouds rolled
back, the sun peeked through, throwing its rays across the mist,
forming the most dramatic, beautiful, colorful rainbow they had
ever seen—complete, from horizon to horizon.

Mom later reported that at that point, she and Dad pulled the
car off the roadway to pray and cry together. They felt the rainbow
was God's way of telling them Skylar would be all right. A few minutes later, their cell phone rang and our pastor delivered the good
news of Skylar's safe delivery. With a sigh of relief and tears of joy
they continued the journey.

Of course, I didn't know about the rainbow until my parents arrived, but I had seen a partial rainbow outside my recovery room window. Another couple visiting us had seen it, too. We had all witnessed the rainbow and felt God's whisper of love in it. Only later would we understand its significance.

While I viewed Skylar through the neonatal unit window for the first time, the neonatologist carefully explained all the details. It was actually four days before we could even cradle him in our hands, and the nurse who gave lots of instructions warned, "If he begins to hiccup, put him down, because that's a sign he is overstimulated."

After forty-eight hours, the doctors felt safe in discussing plans for our son's care. Each day, Skylar grew stronger and healthier. Even though he was small, we could tell he was a high-spirited little boy. The Scripture that kept coming to my mind was 2 Corinthians 12:9: "And He has said to me, 'My grace is sufficient for you, for power is perfected in weakness.'"

Skylar finally came home with us after two months, weighing three pounds, fourteen ounces. We could tell that our son was not at all mentally retarded as the doctors had initially feared. Today at age five, he is developmentally on target—still small but steadily gaining—and the doctors are pleased.

Having a premature baby survive was an incredible blessing, but that event combined with other factors enlarged my heart to prepare for another new beginning. It showed me how God can take painful happenings from our past, add them to the present, and weave them all together for good.

I never dreamed God would use Skylar's birth to remind me of times in my own childhood when a distant relative had secretly molested me. When our doctor had suggested abortion for Skylar, I suddenly realized how easy it would be for any young woman pregnant out of wedlock to abort her baby. I wondered what I would have done as a teenager had that happened to me. With Skylar so tiny, I could just imagine the heartache of that decision.

Even though I thought I had forgiven my hurtful past, through Beth Moore's Bible study *Breaking Free*[1] I recognized that I, like many others, had lived with unconscious shame. Without realizing it, I had imprisoned myself with feelings of inadequacy. When I finally understood that God did not want me to live with that shame and it was not mine to carry, I let it go. My newfound freedom energized me with hope and confidence. As a result, I developed an enthusiastic desire to reach teenage girls in similar circumstances. The sanctity of life for both young and old became a fresh theme in my heart.

All of these events, combined with Keith's background and ministry interest, led us to develop a vision for The Master's Touch Maternity Home. After much prayer, planning, financial support, and community volunteer effort, the home opened its doors in January of 2002 with our mission: *To establish a safe refuge where broken and hurting girls can receive forgiveness and God's grace and be made whole again by the touch of the Master's hand. The Master's Touch strives to see lives changed by ministering to the physical, emotional, and spiritual needs of every individual. Our ultimate goal is to show compassion and love to these girls and to help give the gift of life to their unborn children.*

It amazes me to see what the Lord has done! By His grace, the first occupant of the home is doing well and her baby has safely arrived. And just think—all this is happening as a result of some very painful experiences. I know God has a plan for our little son, Skylar, and now when I see a rainbow, I think about the many other little babies who will be given the opportunity to live and to know their Creator, too.

Faithlifter
Grace

In Her Shoes

Denise is a living illustration of the way only God can redeem a painful situation. She could have continued her life as a *victim*, but through her relationship with Christ and the study of His Word, she allowed God's grace to become operative in her heart and, consequently, became an *overcomer*. She expresses appreciation for her loving parents and also credits her husband, Keith, who encouraged her spiritual growth at a critical time.

Skylar's birth, and the difficulties surrounding it, became a catalyst to seal the couple's relationship and prepare them to dream together toward establishing a home for unwed mothers. Denise's story is a picture of beauty from ashes in many respects.

How has God extended His grace in your life? What areas still need His healing touch?

Are you willing to receive His grace today and look to the future?

In His Word

The Greek word *charis* refers to graciousness, lovingkindness, and goodwill, especially in regard to divine favor and God's redemptive mercy. Here are some insights about grace, God's unmerited favor at Christ's expense:

Grace comes from God the Father.

"For our proud confidence is this: the testimony of our conscience, that in holiness and godly sincerity, not in fleshly wisdom but in the grace of God, we have conducted ourselves in the world, and especially toward you" (2 Corinthians 1:12).

Christ received God's grace.

"The Child continued to grow and become strong, increasing in wisdom; and the grace of God was upon Him" (Luke 2:40).

We receive grace from Christ.

"I am amazed that you are so quickly deserting Him who called you by the grace of Christ, for a different gospel; which is really not another; only there are some who are disturbing you and want to distort the gospel of Christ" (Galatians 1:6-7).

"But the gift is not like the trespass. For if the many died by the trespass of the one man, how much more did God's grace and the gift that came by the grace of the one man, Jesus Christ, overflow to the many!" (Romans 5:15, NIV).

"And God is able to make all grace abound to you, so that always having all sufficiency in everything, you may have an abundance for every good deed" (2 Corinthians 9:8).

"Therefore let us draw near with confidence to the throne of grace, so that we may receive mercy and find grace to help in time of need" (Hebrews 4:16).

"But He gives a greater grace. Therefore it says, 'GOD IS OPPOSED TO THE PROUD, BUT GIVES GRACE TO THE HUMBLE'" (James 4:6).

"But grow in the grace and knowledge of our Lord and Savior Jesus Christ. To Him be the glory, both now and to the day of eternity. Amen" (2 Peter 3:18).

IN YOUR LIFE

What does it mean to walk in grace? God's grace is like opening a beautiful big box wrapped with lovely paper and colorful ribbons. It arrives just when you need it most. Open it and look inside to find three precious gifts:

A blanket—Grace means you can forgive yourself.
We are all sinners, members of the human race, and we have missed the mark in some way. Sometimes we carry heavy loads of guilt, at

times even false guilt, and we are filled with shame. His grace enables us to confess, heal, learn from past mistakes, and look toward the future with hope. What great comfort and encouragement!

Perhaps in your despair over the past you think that such things as sexual sins or abortion could be not be covered by God's grace. However, in her book *Deceived by Shame, Desired by God*, professional counselor Cynthia Humbert wrote: "God is able to heal even the most damaged heart brought before Him. He is the real answer to our painful problems, and He can work in ways we simply don't think are possible. God can, and will, give a woman peace and freedom from a past abortion."[2]

In his book *The Life God Blesses*, Jim Cymbala says: "Faith in Christ is the victory that overcomes not only the world but every engrained sin of the flesh. It doesn't matter how far we have gone, or how deeply the stains of sin have penetrated—the mercy of God is unlimited in its power and scope."[3]

As Denise found in her life, God's grace not only covers our sins and the sins of others against us, but it empowers us to face and respond to life's unexpected events with strength, boldness, and purpose.

A pair of glasses—Grace means you see things from a different perspective.

In his book *What's So Amazing About Grace?* Philip Yancey wrote: "What does a grace-full Christian look like? Perhaps I should rephrase the question, How does a grace-full Christian look? The Christian life, I believe, does not primarily center on ethics or rules but rather involves a new way of seeing. I escape the force of spiritual 'gravity' when I begin to see myself as a sinner who cannot please God by any method of self-improvement or self-enlargement. Only then can I turn to God for outside help—for grace—and to my amazement I learn that a holy God already loves me despite my defects. I escape the force of gravity again when I recognize my neighbors also as sinners, loved by God. A grace-full Christian is one who looks at the world through 'grace-tinted lenses.' "[4]

A kaleidoscope—Grace accommodates itself to whatever you need.
The twists and turns of life are sometimes very difficult to comprehend—the sudden death of a friend, the loss of a spouse through death or divorce, a child gone astray, an accident, injuries, surgery, job loss—and the list goes on. Just as a kaleidoscope rotates to display different and colorful formations, so we can rest in His mercy and grace designed to carry us through each bend in the road.

When we understand more about grace, it lightens our load. This passage reassures us that God takes care of us when we rest in His grace: "Are you tired? Worn out? Burned out on religion? Come to me. Get away with me and you'll recover your life. I'll show you how to take a real rest. Walk with me and work with me—watch how I do it. Learn the unforced rhythms of grace. I won't lay anything heavy or ill-fitting on you. Keep company with me and you'll learn to live freely and lightly" (Matthew 11:28-29, MSG).

Be a grace-giver.
Now that you've unwrapped your gift of grace, you can share it. As Denise experienced different aspects of God's grace in her own life, she reached out to others. The more we learn about grace, the more grateful and amazed we become. As Philip Yancey says, "Grace does not excuse the sin, but it treasures the sinner."[5]

Grace was in God's plan from the beginning of time, but it takes us a lifetime to grasp even a limited vision of all that it means. Like part of a picture painted on canvas, this story highlights a hue in the mural of God's grace.

Now I am humming the old hymn lyrics: "Grace, grace, God's grace. Grace that is greater than all our sin."[6]

CHAPTER NINE

A Guide in the Wilderness

Elaine Hamilton

"The tumor is malignant, inoperable."

Our doctor's pronouncement carved a crater in my soul. Although we knew the possibilities, I couldn't believe it.

Malignant? Inoperable? Am I dreaming? I almost felt detached from reality as I heard the doctor describe my forty-six-year-old husband's brain tumor. *How could this be happening to us?* Bob had just completed his doctorate. As a local pastor for fourteen years, he had earned the loving respect of his twelve-hundred-member flock. We had cherished twenty-five years of marriage and nurtured close relationships with our daughter, Scarlett, now in college, and our son, Patrick, a high school senior. I wondered, *What lies ahead? How will I cope?*

For the next several months, we worked together. Because he was too weak to spend hours reading, preparing, and writing out his sermons, he lay in bed and jotted a few notes while listening to me read selections from the Bible and commentaries. Finally, after completing a series of radiation therapy, Bob gained enough strength to preach on the topic of heaven. But it wasn't easy.

When we arrived at church, I helped him into his study, attached the microphone, and walked him to the door of the worship center. As I let go and watched him plod to the podium during a prayer, helplessness hit me like a wave. *How can he preach a sermon from that small set of notes?* I thought. But the Holy Spirit gave him fervor as he stood behind the pulpit with dignity and poise during his last sermon.

"God is good," Bob emphasized with supernatural strength, "and God is the same yesterday, today, and forever." The testimony of Bob's life spoke louder than words. He sat in a tall chair after the service while people in the congregation stood in line to hug him and express their love.

Perhaps I was in denial, but I really expected a miraculous healing. We continued to get medical opinions, but all the conferences ended with the same conclusion: "There is nothing more we can do." As a last resort, Bob decided to try chemotherapy treatments offered in Dallas. As his weakness accelerated, home-health nurses administered his care; Bob insisted I continue my job teaching high school English.

Very early one morning when I arose to read him our customary devotional, I found Bob unresponsive. His breathing seemed more relaxed after hearing me, but when I looked down, tears trickled along the sides of his face. I blotted his cheeks and wondered what he was thinking. Within the hour, he had died. The children and I embraced and wept together.

Although I'd known Christ since childhood, I had never felt so forsaken. Through the years as my pastor, Bob had faithfully taught me to rely on the character of God. Now came the test. Would He be there for me? I drew strength from the reassurance that God is a husband to the widow and a father to the fatherless (see Psalm 146:9; Isaiah 54:5). But I never dreamed my children and I would be the ones in need.

As I entered the wilderness of widowhood in the months following Bob's death, I felt cushioned by the Lord's grace and the loving care of my family, church family, and close friends, but for the first time, I was alone. Both children went away to college, thanks to a scholarship fund established by the church. My teaching job kept me active, but instead of having Bob there to share my life with at the end of a busy day, the house echoed with quietness. In the silence, I felt the very essence of myself being stripped away.

Everything I had been accustomed to and had enjoyed—preparing meals, housekeeping, being wife and mother—was no longer the same. Bob and I had always anticipated our regular lunch date on Friday. Now I dreaded Fridays; they were too painful. I missed so many traditions that had become a part of my life.

I struggled to find my identity. I had enjoyed my role as a pastor's wife, feeling it was my way of honoring the Lord. Now it was difficult for me to go to church. When I did, I cried through most of the service. I kept hoping I would see Bob walking around the corner; when he wasn't there, the emptiness grew to a piercing void. I prayed about moving my membership, but the Lord quietly said, "Stay." It helped me to know that people had not forgotten the one who was always on my mind.

I knew I needed to go to the Lord—to pray and to stay in His Word—but sometimes I rebelled and felt sorry for myself. The results sent me deeper into the pit of despair; school papers were not graded on time, and I was overcome with anxiety.

When I resisted the Lord, I could almost hear Bob's voice resounding, "To one who knows the right thing to do and does not do it, to him it is sin" (James 4:17). Conviction reminded me that I needed to obey the Lord and not give in to my feelings.

I remembered what our British friend Dr. J. Sidlow Baxter once said: "Prayerlessness is a spiritual grave." In his book *Does God Still Guide?* I read, "When prayer becomes a dear delight of communication, its reflex influence upon the human mind is wonderfully healing and exhilarating. It releases the nervous system from tensions, relieves the mind from pressures, restores a true sense of values in life, and refreshes one's whole organism. It is then that we begin to hear in our deepest consciousness the soul music of such promises as Isaiah 26:3, 'Thou wilt keep him in perfect peace, whose mind is stayed on thee'; and Psalm 91:1, 'He that dwelleth in the secret place of the most High shall abide under the shadow of the Almighty'; and Philippians 4:7, 'The peace of God, which passes all understanding.'"[1]

Dr. Baxter's words renewed my passion to wait upon the Lord and listen for His personal message to me. I felt the Lord saying, "Life on earth has ended for Bob, but I still have plans for you."

"But, Lord," I argued, "sometimes I don't feel like pressing on." Yet I wanted more than anything to become the person Christ wanted me to be. One day while driving alone, I began thinking of how I had relied upon Bob for spiritual leadership. Now he was gone. Tears flowed as I talked with God. "Lord, you know how disappointed I am that you didn't heal Bob. Today I want to thank you for dying for me, for loving me as an individual. And Your Word says that You are now my husband and I can trust You to provide for my needs. You are my provider, my sustainer, my life."

Suddenly I sensed intimacy, oneness, and peace. From that day on, I decided to keep moving forward and entrust my life to Him, even though, like Job, I felt I'd been slain.

The Lord was ready to guide me, but I had to become a determined follower. I decided to be a positive person and the best mother I could be. I couldn't fill their father's place, but I could pray for wisdom in how to counsel my grown children. They gave me a will to live.

I knew I would have to accept the fact that my lifestyle would never be the same, but I resolved through the Lord's strength that I would make it alone. As a widow I felt socially awkward, but some couples in the church helped by asking me to sit with them. When I needed advice and help, the right person appeared.

Occasionally I had to deal with the fear of living alone, but I decided, *Lord, since You provided this home for me, I will trust You to take care of me while I am in it.* Bob and I had built our rural home together, and we both loved it. I wanted to stay.

Sometimes doubts needled me regarding Bob's illness. Were our decisions right? One day I reached a point of resolution. The thought came to me as though the Lord were speaking. *I love you. I am the sovereign Lord of the universe, and I am not treating you like a mean, earthly father would. I have your best interest at heart.* I responded by saying, "Lord, we were in Your hands. You allowed Bob to die. I need not understand why."

Holidays the first year left me limp, but even then, God was near. Christmas was especially hard, but we received a package from our friend Connie in North Carolina: "Enclosed are some special gifts for you I think Bob would have liked. Someone shared gifts with me when I lost my husband, and I wanted to do the same for you and the children. Love, Connie."

Connie's thoughtfulness meant so much that I began thinking of ways I could reach out to others. On Bob's birthday, I did not place flowers on his grave, but sent a fragrant yellow rose (Bob's favorite flower) to his mother in North Carolina, remembering that she had lost a husband and two of her children.

In the passing years since Bob's death, the Lord has guided me through prayer, His Word, and the words and actions of dear friends.

I have rejoiced to see the Lord provide godly mates for both Scarlett and Patrick, as well as the blessing of grandchildren. The Lord sometimes even leads me through the suggestions and insights of my gracious young family. (Sometimes they send *me* a yellow rose.)

I'm learning that it doesn't matter who we are or what we look like on the outside; each one of us needs encouragement. Bob was a great encourager because he believed in the truth and power of God's Word to change us. Now I feel the Lord nudging me to follow his example, letting others know that in the loneliest times of our lives, Jesus whispers, "I'm here. I love you. You'll make it."

"And the LORD will continually guide you, and satisfy your desire in scorched places, and give strength to your bones; and you will be like a watered garden, and like a spring of water whose waters do not fail" (Isaiah 58:11).

Faithlifter
Obedience

IN HER SHOES

Elaine experienced the loss of her husband, but she also lost her pastor. She relied heavily upon his spiritual strength, but when he left earth for heaven, Elaine struggled to make her faith her own. Even if you have not experienced the death of a spouse, can you relate to some of Elaine's spiritual struggles, especially in regard to obedience? Have you ever been tempted to trust in your emotions rather than in God's Word?

Elaine learned that as she obeyed the Lord, she gained strength to obey again. As she listened to God's voice, she experienced peace and recognized His guidance. Her relationship with God did not depend upon her pastor-husband, but became very personal and, ultimately, very powerful. Have you ever found yourself leaning on someone else's words instead of going directly to His Word?

Have you struggled with doing what you know the Lord wants you to do?

IN HIS WORD

To obey means to willingly carry out the orders of someone, to submit, or to be guided by one's conscience or by the Holy Spirit. The Hebrew word for *obedience* has three shades of meaning: to hear intelligently, to see reason, and to act in accord with the reason perceived.

Faith is tucked away inside the heart, but obedience is the outward expression of that faith and may be observed by others. When a person obeys God, she is showing that she truly believes. We believe because we are persuaded that something is true.

Here are some ideas from specific Scriptures about obedience:

Circumstances will test our obedience.

"When troubles come and all these awful things happen to you, in future days you will come back to GOD, your God, and listen obediently to what he says. GOD, your God, is above all a compassionate God. In the end he will not abandon you, he won't bring you to ruin, he won't forget the covenant with your ancestors which he swore to them" (Deuteronomy 4:30-31, MSG).

Disobedience has consequences.

" 'If you consent and obey, you will eat the best of the land; but if you refuse and rebel, you will be devoured by the sword.' Truly, the mouth of the LORD has spoken" (Isaiah 1:19-20).

"Do not be deceived, God is not mocked; for whatever a man sows, this he will also reap" (Galatians 6:7).

Jesus is our example of obedience.

"Although He was a Son, He learned obedience from the things which He suffered. And having been made perfect, He became to all those who obey Him the source of eternal salvation" (Hebrews 5:8-9).

"We are destroying speculations and every lofty thing raised up against the knowledge of God, and we are taking every thought captive to the obedience of Christ" (2 Corinthians 10:5).

IN YOUR LIFE

How can these verses be applied to everyday living? Here are a few suggestions:

Be sensitive to God's leading.

Do you ever have a problem with procrastination? Sometimes I hear what God is saying, but I argue that I'll do it later. That's not right. Obedience is simply doing what God wants us to do *right then*. Just as human law punishes civil disobedience, there are spiritual consequences to disobedience against God. Probably the most devastating is that our fellowship with Him is hindered and we become spiritually stagnant. The question is, *Will I seek to live life my way or God's way?*

Habitually trust God and do what He says.

Author Elisabeth Elliot wrote in her journal after the death of her second husband: "I find that routine is the best support for my soul. I can function with almost customary efficiency and concentration, so long as I operate by habit—the sameness, ordinariness, and necessity are comforting. It is in the interruption of routine that I find myself beginning to disintegrate and turn inward. That is hazardous, and I have to take the reins firmly and say 'giddap!' "[2]

Obedience is just finding the next thing God wants you to do, and then doing it.

Prepare to be a blessing and to receive a blessing!

God has promised to bless obedience, and we will be rewarded in due time. When the apostle Paul wrote from his jail cell to friends in Philippi, he said, "When I was living among you, you lived in responsive obedience. Now that I'm separated from you, keep it up. . . . Go out into the world uncorrupted, a breath of fresh air in this squalid and polluted society. Provide people with a glimpse of good living and of the living God. Carry the light-giving Message into the night so I'll have good cause to be proud of you on the day that Christ returns" (Philippians 2:12-18, MSG).

Perhaps you have found, as Elaine did, that obedience is an act of love for God. Again we see the relationship between love and trust. We trust that God will do what He says, but in His time and according to His plan, not ours.

Charles Haddon Spurgeon wrote, "Faith and obedience are bound up in the same bundle. He that obeys God, trusts God; and he that trusts God, obeys God."[3]

Oswald Chambers observed, "The best measure of a spiritual life is not its ecstasies but its obedience."[4]

CHAPTER TEN

My Search for Yeshua

Julie Rand

Single at twenty-two, I ran a successful business in Beverly Hills, California, designing and maintaining window mannequin displays for forty high-fashion stores. With my generous income I purchased pricey clothes, a car, furniture, whatever I wanted. Yet my consumer lifestyle left me feeling empty and shallow, and I kept wondering, *What is missing?*

One day I noticed a pink antique crystal vase on my antique dining table and thought, *If that expensive glassware breaks . . . so what? It has no lasting value. What is really important, anyway?* (see Matthew 16:26).

Thoughts of childhood reminded me that my orthodox Jewish grandmother had planted seeds of spiritual interest. I had accompanied my grandparents to the synagogue monthly, but my middle-class Gentile father and Jewish mother had said, "You and your sister can make up your own minds about religion." Although we didn't attend church, I sometimes opened a large, coffee-table family Bible and studied the impressive, colorful illustrations. I knew God must be somewhere because every night when I looked at the stars and smelled the roses outside my window, I felt sure He had made them and that He knew me.

While in junior high, I had focused on good grades, artwork, and dancing, but more than anything, I wanted to have a happier home life. Unfortunately, I chose friends with similar family problems (figuring, I guess, that they would understand), and I began drinking with them. They were a negative influence in many ways (see 1 Corinthians 15:33). Finally at one party I told my friends, "I'm leaving. I don't want to do these things anymore."

After college, my artistic talents paid off in a lucrative career, but my lifestyle slipped back into friendships with those engaging in deeds of darkness. This time it took several years and various situations to bring me to a turning point. One experience was particularly significant in my turnaround.

Prior to my financial success, I had temporarily driven a school bus for extremely handicapped children. I was so impressed when mothers with smiling faces and peaceful countenances came out to meet their children. They radiated so much joy. Because most of the families lived in the stench of poverty, I had to wonder, *Did they possess something I didn't have?*

Now, several years later, while sitting in my comfortable surroundings, I thought about those women and felt an unexplainable urge to sell everything and give it to the poor (see Luke 18:22)— which I did. Within a week, I had dismantled my elegant home and sold everything except my car, sewing machine, bike, and a few essentials. One evening at a Halloween party, I made my choice, said good-bye to my friends, and set out to find God and meaning in life.

My search took me to Santa Cruz, where I began working in a health food store, did some cooking, and sewed costumes. I tried yoga, palm reading, tarot cards, vegetarian diets, and conversing with various gurus. "Why should people bow down to you?" I would ask. "Aren't you just a man?" Their responses never satisfied me. All the Eastern religious meditation methods were dead-end roads. After ten years, nothing filled the emptiness in my soul.

My pursuit continued as I traveled to Juneau, Alaska, where my gypsy-like appearance caught the attention of Mick Ewing, a young man who asked, "Can you join us for dinner tonight? My wife, Sherri, and I would like to invite you." He added, "Others will be coming, too."

That evening in their modest home, Mick and Sherri extended unconditional love to a small group of singles. After a simple meal, we sat around listening to guitar music and singing. When Mick began teaching from the Bible, my heart felt calmed, warm, and secure. Hearing God's words touched me deeply. Something inside said, *This is Truth. Listen carefully.*

Mick taught about important areas that applied to me every day as a young woman—lifestyle, attitudes, holiness, and purity. I needed help with all those things. And then he taught from Matthew 7:13-14, "Enter through the narrow gate. For wide is the gate and broad is the road that leads to destruction, and many enter through it. But small is the gate and narrow the road that leads to life, and only a few find it" (NIV).

He said something like, "We have all sinned, and we cannot keep God's moral laws so we need a redeemer, God's son, Jesus, Messiah." He explained that we each need a personal relationship with God, and that God loved us so much that while we were still sinners, Messiah died for us (see Romans 5:8). For the first time I understood that Yeshua (Hebrew for Jesus) became the perfect Passover Lamb, shedding His blood and dying in my place, giving me life forever in heaven.

That night I saw my imperfect life compared to a perfect God. I asked God to forgive my sins, and with a repentant heart, I placed my trust in Yeshua. At last I was free! I had found the spiritual riches money cannot buy. The verse in Jeremiah 29:13 had come true: "You will seek me and find me when you seek me with all your heart" (NIV). I thought, *Now I have the answer for which I've been searching these past ten years!* The Lord showed me that even though there is no longer a temple in Jerusalem, my body is a temple for the Holy Spirit. He lives inside me and gives me the power to overcome evil desires and become the person He designed me to be.

Mick and Sherri invited me to stay in their Discipleship Home for young women who were new believers, but only if I would abide by their rules, including refraining from alcohol and drugs. When I accepted the challenge, God began changing my life through Bible study, prayer, and fellowship. After one year of working and studying, I eagerly returned to the Lower 48 with a desire to share good news about the Lord with my family and friends.

Then, while attending a Jewish believers' retreat in 1985, I met Ron Rand, another messianic Jew from Los Angeles. Our relationship deepened as we studied and witnessed together; in 1987 we were married and in 1990 moved to Texas. Then in 1993, Ron's skills as a senior engineer specialist gave us the opportunity to work in Israel, so we took our infant son, Josiah, and moved to Tiberias.

That year both humbled me and tested my faith. In addition to culture shock and language barriers, I adjusted to life without an air conditioner, heater, dishwasher, or clothes dryer. We had no carpeted floors so I mopped almost every day, often finding scorpions in our rooms. I walked to the market and on the way home hoisted the baby on one hip and the groceries on the other. I often struggled with discouragement as I learned, like Paul, to be content in my circumstances, whatever they might be.

Even though Ron and I were both Jewish and applied for citizenship, it was not granted. When people would ask, "How can you be Jewish and be denied citizenship?" we would answer, "Because we believe Yeshua is the Messiah." However, the rejection became an opportunity for us to share with many the New Covenant (Brit Hadashah). During those days, Ron and I prayed for protection as we could almost feel the spiritual forces battling around us. To stand firm, we clutched our Bibles more closely, studied and prayed diligently, and continued to claim God's promises.

Since returning to the States, Ron and I have felt God calling us to assist Gentiles in understanding the first five books of the Bible and their significance to believers. We are providing classes and opportunities to help prepare the bride of Christ for His Second Coming and to help Gentile Christians better understand the meaning of Passover and other Jewish feasts and traditions that Jesus Himself observed while on earth.

We attend a messianic congregation, Eitz Chaim (which means Tree of Life), and feel burdened for our Jewish friends. Now that I have found my Yeshua, I want others to find Him, too.

Faithlifter
Trust

IN HER SHOES

Because of Julie's Jewish background, caring heart, and gift of hospitality, she is now able to help others understand more about the life of Jesus and the feasts He observed. Have you considered the significance of our Jewish heritage and how we Gentiles are "grafted" into God's family? Julie and her family occasionally open their home to give demonstrations of these observances and explain their significance in the Christian walk today.

Julie's extended search for meaning in life represents thousands who are immersed in the same dilemma. The voids in their hearts are not filled after experimenting with all sorts of worldly "isms." How did God use childhood experiences to plant seeds in Julie's heart? How were those seeds nourished? Have you, like Julie, ever embarked on a search for a fulfilling life? Have you found it?

IN HIS WORD

Trusting is such an everyday experience that we don't even think about it. We trust the pilot who flies the plane, the driver who drives the bus, the engineer who designs the bridge, the plumber who fixes the leak, the surgeon who stitches our bodies. These people have expertise in their respective fields of endeavor, and we trust they have prepared and studied to do the best job they can. We trust them temporarily, but we trust God for eternity.

The Hebrew word for the verb *trust* means "to have confidence in." Here are a few Scriptures that enlarge upon this concept and assure us that God is worthy of our trust:

"Trust in the LORD with all your heart and do not lean on your own understanding. In all your ways acknowledge Him, and He will make your paths straight" (Proverbs 3:5-6).

"It is better to take refuge in the LORD than to trust in man" (Psalm 118:8).

"He who gives attention to the word will find good, and blessed is he who trusts in the LORD" (Proverbs 16:20).

"An arrogant man stirs up strife, but he who trusts in the LORD will prosper" (Proverbs 28:25).

"You who fear the LORD, trust in the LORD; He is their help and their shield" (Psalm 115:11).

"Commit your way to the LORD, trust also in Him, and He will do it" (Psalm 37:5).

"In God I have put my trust, I shall not be afraid. What can man do to me?" (Psalm 56:11).

"Some trust in chariots and some in horses, but we trust in the name of the LORD our God" (Psalm 20:7, NIV).

IN YOUR LIFE

Get to know God through His Word.

Our trust in God becomes secure as we get to know Him and His divine plan for us as revealed in Genesis to Revelation. Ron and Julie helped me learn more about the Jewish feasts. Perhaps you would be interested in learning a few facts about Rosh Hashanah, the Jewish New Year.

A blast on the shofar, or ram's horn, is the central focus and represents God's provision of the ram as a sacrifice when Abraham, acting in obedience, had taken Isaac to Mount Moriah for that same purpose (see Genesis 22:1-19). That account prophesied the sacrifice of the Messiah in the New Testament (see Luke 23). The ram's horn at Rosh Hashanah acts as a wake-up call for us to be alert and ready for the coming of the King (see 1 Thessalonians 4:16-17). For ten days the people repent, examine, and evaluate their lives.

At the feast that closes Rosh Hashanah, the finest silver and crystal set the table as if a king were coming to dinner. The hostess wears white, the tablecloth is white, and even the food and the way it is served has significance. For example, the bread is baked in a circle to symbolize a king's crown, and the dish of apples and honey represents the hope of sweetness in the New Year.

Studying the Bible and gaining more information about it is like digging out precious nuggets from the gold mine of truth. The story of our Jewish friends who discovered that Jesus is the Messiah helps illuminate our understanding of the connections between the Old Testament and the New.

Study the character of God.

Trusting God involves concentrating on the object of our trust. A few years ago my husband, Jim, and I took sailing lessons. The gems of instruction we received in the classroom did not become completely clear to us until we set sail. For instance, a boat anchor is not adequately tested in the harbor. It is during the storm—when the waves are crashing in and the boat is pitching in all directions—that the integrity of the anchor is tested. Likewise, it is during our times of depression or despair that we can truly know God's faithfulness. God is our anchor of hope. He is for us and He never fails.

When reading your Bible, note in the margin each time one of God's character traits—Loving, Holy, Faithful, Compassionate, Merciful, Immutable (unchanging), Omnipresent (always present everywhere), Omniscient (all-wise), Omnipotent (all-powerful), Just, Supreme—is demonstrated. Knowing God is essential to our faith.

Rely upon His sovereignty.

Our adult son recently was diagnosed with cystic fibrosis. While most cases are detected early in infancy, his particular genetic makeup did not alarm the doctors to test for the disease until symptoms were manifested in adulthood. We are told that scenario accounts for about 10 percent of patients with the disease. Initially we were devastated, but now we feel encouraged by research and new medications for extending life expectancy. We pray daily for our son and are thankful that he knows the Lord and is growing in faith.

Sometimes it is difficult to trust God. Things are not always as we want them to be. Our trust is put to the test when a loved one dies, a severely handicapped child is born, we hear a poor diagnosis, a husband loses his job, or a terrorist attacks. *Where is God? Does He care? Can I really trust Him?*

In his book *When God Doesn't Make Sense*, Dr. James Dobson wrote, "Apparently, most believers are permitted to go through emotional and spiritual valleys that are designed to test their faith in the crucible of fire. Why? Because faith ranks at the top of God's system of priorities. And what is faith? It is 'the substance of things hoped for, the evidence of things not seen' (Hebrews 11:1, KJV). This determination to believe when the proof is not provided and when the questions are not answered is central to our relationship with the Lord. He will never do anything to destroy the need for faith. In fact, He guides us through times of testing specifically to cultivate that belief and dependence on Him (Hebrews 11:6-7)."[1]

Rather than being offended by God's sovereignty, we should be comforted by it because we know that the very nature of God is love and that He desires what is best for His children. Sometimes we get impatient and forget that God's sovereignty works behind the scenes (to deliver His people, such as through Esther's courage) as well as in more dramatic ways (as with the parting of the Red Sea).

Author Jerry Bridges adds, "We honor God by choosing to trust Him when we don't understand what He is doing or why He has allowed some adverse circumstance to occur. As we seek God's glory, we may be sure that He has purposed our good and that He will not be frustrated in fulfilling that purpose."[2]

Faith and trust are intertwined. As declared in Romans 15:4, "For everything that was written in the past was written to teach us, so that through endurance and the encouragement of the Scriptures we might have hope" (NIV).

To experience this comfort and encouragement, we will need to trust God and to live, as Paul said, "by faith, not by sight" (2 Corinthians 5:7).

CHAPTER ELEVEN

When All You Have Left Is Jesus

Carolann Conley

My husband, Doc, and I reared our three sons in a moral environment, supported their school activities, and welcomed their friends. We all attended church together. Doc spent time with each of our sons as they were growing up while I enjoyed being "Mom" and keeping our house in some semblance of order. Eventually, Scotty, Steve, and John moved out and went their separate ways, but it seemed our home had a revolving door. Steve and John each came back at different times to stay.

It was only after the boys left that Doc and I moved, found a great church, experienced spiritual renewal, and launched a spiritual journey that drew us closer to each other and closer to God. I chose Proverbs 3:5-6 as my life verses and began to trust God every day. When serious testing of our faith began, Doc and I prayed together and asked the Lord to guide us through one horrible mess after another. At times it seemed the situation could not get any worse, and then it did.

Steve joined the marines after high school graduation and became involved with a young woman who later gave birth to their daughter.

The marriage didn't last, and after the divorce, Steve delved into drug and alcohol abuse to dull the pain. With his thinking clouded, he went AWOL, but at the time, we couldn't understand why.

After we were notified, Doc called Steve's commanding officer and said, "When I was an officer in the navy, the military police went after the AWOL guys and brought them back."

The officer flatly stated, "We don't do that anymore."

One night a few weeks before Christmas, the phone rang and Doc sat on the living room floor with the telephone in his lap, tears streaming down his cheeks as he answered, "No, Son, you cannot come. If you do, I'll have to turn you in to the authorities."

Steve was asking to come home for Christmas, and it just killed Doc to say no. But he would not compromise his own integrity and his military background. Doc urged Steve to cooperate. Finally, Steve turned himself in and spent some time in the brig.

Each time my spirit would sink, I read the Psalms for comfort: "The Lord is close to those whose hearts are breaking; he rescues those who are humbly sorry for their sins. The good man does not escape all troubles—he has them too. But the Lord helps him in each and every one" (Psalm 34:18-19, TLB).

After his military service discharge, Steve moved to another community close by and eventually married again, another bad choice. A few years later, he divorced a second time, and we sadly said good-bye to a second granddaughter. Without the Lord in my life, I could not have faced another day. We were so disappointed.

Our youngest son, John, diagnosed with a terminal illness, tried to kill himself three times and had also turned to drug and alcohol abuse. While Doc and I told our two boys we did not approve of their lifestyles, we became an emotional safety net for them because of our love.

After John's third suicide attempt, we visited him at the psychiatric hospital. When the attendant unlocked a heavy steel door, the eerie clanging made me shudder, and I cringed as the grinding metal crash locked it behind us. There we visited with John and encouraged him to look ahead and plan his future. He said he wanted to continue his education, so after his release, we invited him to move back home temporarily, with the stipulation that he would complete his college degree. He accepted our offer, eventually graduated, and moved to a nearby city after accepting a good position with an insurance company.

As a couple, Doc and I leaned on each other and our love grew as we moved from one crisis to the next. When the swinging door of our home seemed unending, we just pulled together and talked through our feelings. We didn't blame each other for what was happening. I felt sad for Doc as a father and he agonized for me as a mother, but we continued to seek the Lord's wisdom.

Doc was forced to take a medical retirement because of vascular problems, and further complications led to the amputation of his right leg. It took several months for him to adjust to his prosthesis, and during that time my work load increased.

I couldn't quote Scripture exactly, but I knew the main principles, so I walked around the house talking with God using my own paraphrase. I felt like a "Martha" with too much to do (described in Luke 10:38-42), but sometimes I would just close my eyes and envision Jesus and dwell upon the wonderful fact that regardless of what was happening, Jesus knew and He loved me. That was all that really mattered. Often when reading the Psalms, I read aloud as if it were a letter from the Lord to me:

Dear Carolann,
"In your day of trouble, may the Lord be with you! . . .
May there be shouts of joy when we hear the news of your victory, flags flying with praise to God for all that he has done for you. May he answer all your prayers!"
(Psalm 20:1-5, TLB).
—Your loving Father

In the meantime, John called Doc almost every day to encourage him after his amputation and, as a result, they became very close. Only the Lord could have sustained us through John's subsequent AIDS-related death in 1986 and all the details surrounding that event. Most of our friends did not even know John's diagnosis because Doc and I were so devastated by it that for years we kept it a secret. Hiding it was a burden almost too great to bear.

We were still reeling from that grief when Steve became ill with cirrhosis of the liver because of his drug and alcohol excesses. He was experiencing his third failed marriage, and we said good-bye to yet another granddaughter.

One day at church a friend said, "Carolann, you don't know what an inspiration you've been with all you and Doc have been through." I appreciated her compliment, but could take no credit whatsoever. God was working in me and it was just a normal thing, like breathing, as I relied on Him for strength.

I felt pressed to the limit and didn't know how much more adversity I could take, but the Lord sustained me through His Word: "Don't be impatient. Wait for the Lord, and he will come and save you! Be brave, stouthearted and courageous. Yes, wait and he will help you" (Psalm 27:14, TLB). I learned that being courageous is a willful decision, not something that just happens.

Unfortunately, in February of 1992, Steve's liver disease had rapidly progressed to a critical point, and again we said another final good-bye. Each son had made his peace with God before death, but I thought, *As their mother, I was there for our two sons' first breaths, and I was there for their last.* It didn't seem natural that they should die first, but at least I knew they were in a better place. Still, letting go was an indescribable, soul-wrenching experience. A friend told me, "Carolann, the Bible says that God puts our tears in a bottle, but for you He might have to find a five-gallon drum." That said it all!

Doc and I returned to our home with empty hearts, but God gave us quality time together, and for the next few months Doc and I experienced a honeymoon-like retreat. We felt God's comfort and presence as we loved each other and tried to look forward. Even strangers commented on our forty-seven-year love affair.

Then in October of 1992, Doc passed away. So many times during the days that followed, God just seemed to carry me from place to place. Looking back now, I don't know how I made it, and some of the really bad times are blocked from my memory.

Having no siblings, I had the sole responsibility of caring for my aging mother, and finally, after Mama died in 1994, I realized I had not brought any closure to my emotional trauma and grief. God showed me that in order to heal, I needed to go back and work through each death. I had to dump a lot of garbage from my heart—anger, guilt, resentment, and frustration.

When I admitted past issues that haunted me and dealt with them, I could finally rest in God's peace and regain my zest for life, but it took a number of years to reach that point. Scotty, our oldest son, had exemplary behavior and a strong Christian testimony, but he had difficulty dealing with his brothers' problems and felt most comfortable distancing himself from our family. Only in recent times have some of those hurts begun to heal.

Now I have time to be a "Mary" (described in Luke 10:38-42), to be still and listen, and to think about Him bending His ear to me: "I love the Lord because he hears my prayers and answers them. Because he bends down and listens, I will pray as long as I breathe!" (Psalm 116:1-2, TLB).

God continues to answer prayers that I whispered long ago. In traversing all my circumstances, I have learned not to blame God but to know that He loves me, walks alongside me, and feels my pain. Each morning is a new day, and I'm thankful for the blessing of life and the new lessons I'm learning. Encouraging friends include me in activities, and I'm using my homemaking and hospitality talents at various church events. My desire now is to help others who are struggling with life's burdens. Like the apostle Paul I am pressing on to the finish line, and when our eyes are focused ahead, we can't keep looking back.

I can identify with Sheila Walsh, who in her book *Living Fearlessly* describes her little son jumping confidently into her arms: "That's where I want to be with God. I want my life to be a faith-filled leap into his arms, knowing he will be there—not that everything will go as I want, but that *he will be there* and that this will be enough."[1]

All I have left now is Jesus, but after all I've been through, I can truthfully say, "Jesus is all I really need."

Faithlifter
Steadfastness

IN HER SHOES

In his book *Destined for the Cross*, Paul Billheimer states, "God does not make us all at once. The process is a long one, running through all the years of our life. God begins making us when we are born and His work goes on continuously all our days. There is never an hour when some new touch is not given to our life, some new line marked out in our character."[2]

Carolann's account reminds me of the book of Job. Just when she thought nothing else bad could happen, it did. The loss of her family one by one leaves us breathless, not to mention sensing the heartache she must have felt because of her straying sons and the loss of contact with grandchildren. Do you know someone going through similar trials? What could you say to encourage that person? It is clear that Carolann developed character through it all. How did she demonstrate steadfast faith?

IN HIS WORD

The prime time to soak in the truth of God's Word, walk hand in hand with the Father, and grow in fellowship with Him is when everything seems fine and our lives are not engulfed by a crisis. When disappointments come—and they do—we need the reassurance of His loving presence, the knowledge of His ability to care for us, and the certainty of His faithful, tender comfort.

The Greek word for *steadfast* means "to be firm and sure." Similar words denote strength, foundation, and support. I've seen some huge rock mountains, especially in Canada, and boulders that could not be moved or broken, apart from an act of God. Even that word picture is one used in Scripture to describe His steadfast character and the steadfastness we should exhibit because of it.

"So this is what the Sovereign LORD says: 'See, I lay a stone in Zion, a tested stone, a precious cornerstone for a sure foundation; the one who trusts will never be dismayed'" (Isaiah 28:16, NIV).

"You're no longer wandering exiles. This kingdom of faith is now your home country. You're no longer strangers or outsiders. You *belong* here, with as much right to the name Christian as anyone. God is building a home. He's using us all—irrespective of how we got here—in what he is building. He used the apostles and prophets for the foundation. Now he's using you, fitting you in brick by brick, stone by stone, with Christ Jesus as the cornerstone that holds all the parts together. We see it taking shape day after day—a holy temple built by God, all of us built into it, a temple in which God is quite at home" (Ephesians 2:19-22, MSG).

"We have come to share in Christ if we hold firmly till the end the confidence we had at first" (Hebrews 3:14, NIV).

"To You they cried out and were delivered; in You they trusted and were not disappointed" (Psalm 22:5).

"Yet He has now reconciled you in His fleshly body through death, in order to present you before Him holy and blameless and beyond reproach—if indeed you continue in the faith firmly established and steadfast, and not moved away from the hope of the gospel that you have heard, which was proclaimed in all creation under heaven, and of which I, Paul, was made a minister" (Colossians 1:22-23).

"Therefore, my beloved brethren, be steadfast, immovable, always abounding in the work of the Lord, knowing that your toil is not in vain in the Lord" (1 Corinthians 15:58).

IN YOUR LIFE
While your circumstances will likely be different than Carolann's, perhaps you will find these suggestions helpful as you seek to remain steadfast during your trials and tests:

Speak God's Word aloud.
When we are in distress, there is something very soothing about our ears hearing our mouths speak forth the words of God.

Stand firm in Christ.

Just as Carolann chose to cling to the Savior during her trials and brought attention to His faithfulness, we can make that choice as well. When God looks at us, He does not see us standing alone, but united with Christ, clothed in His righteousness, as one of the living stones fixed to Jesus, our Cornerstone. He is faithful, no matter what happens in our lives.

Oswald Chambers wrote: "Believe steadfastly on Him and all you come up against will develop your faith. Faith is unutterable trust in God, trust which never dreams that he will not stand by us."[3]

Let your "will" rule over your emotions.

Human emotional responses are up and down, depending upon the circumstances and how we feel. But when you choose faith in the midst of darkness, your choice becomes a stabilizing force to your heart and a beacon of light to those around you.

In her book *The Christian's Secret of a Happy Life*, Hannah Whitall Smith wrote: "I remember, very early in my Christian life, having every tender and loyal impulse within me stirred to the depths of an appeal I met with in a volume of old sermons, to all who loved the Lord Jesus, that they should show to others how worthy He was of being trusted by the steadfastness of their own faith in Him. As I read the inspiring words, there came to me a sudden glimpse of the privilege and the glory of being called to walk in paths so dark, that only an utter recklessness of trust would be possible!"[4]

Never doubt God's love for you.

I do not believe we can separate our trust in God's steadfastness from the knowledge of God's love. It is easy to trust and have faith when things are going our way, but we are tempted to question and doubt when problems start piling up.

"For as high as the heavens are above the earth, so great is his love for those who fear him" (Psalm 103:11, NIV). About this verse Jerry Bridges says: "Here we see that God's love for His own is as high as the heavens are above the earth. Just as God's wisdom, like the height of the heavens, cannot be measured, so God's love for us cannot be measured. It is not only perfect in its effect, it is infinite in its extent. No calamity that may come upon us, however great it may be, can carry us beyond the pale of God's fatherly love for us."[5]

This knowledge gives us comfort and security, realizing that we have a loving God. If we feel that God is far away, we need to examine our part in the relationship because He said, "I will not forget you. Behold, I have inscribed you on the palms of My hands" (Isaiah 49:15-16). An inscription cannot be erased. Engraving is permanent. I once heard a teenager say that if God had a refrigerator, her picture would be attached to it! Is yours there, too?

CHAPTER TWELVE

Air for the Soul

Elizabeth Garland

"Mrs. Garland, you need to begin using supplemental oxygen twenty-four hours a day," the doctor said thoughtfully as he peered over horn-rimmed glasses.

You know he's right, I thought, but my heart sank at his words. *Lord, please don't allow this*, I pleaded silently. *Look at what I've already been through in my fifty-five years! How can I take more?*

"Mrs. Garland, did you hear me?" the doctor gently prompted.

I looked at my husband, Walter, for his reaction. He nodded to the doctor.

Fear gripped me, but I heard myself calmly respond, "If you say so."

Oxygen assistance was crucial for me. Surgeries following tuberculosis and then a mastectomy had left scar tissue that prevented my lung from expanding enough. I was almost always short of breath. But I wasn't ready to be harnessed to a contraption that would rob me of my independence. While I'd managed to overcome many medical hurdles, this one seemed insurmountable.

My discouragement deepened later that day when the oxygen therapist arrived at our home. I peeked through the curtain when his van pulled in the driveway. I wanted to hide and pretend no one was home.

Walter greeted the young man who brought my breathing apparatus. What a gadget! The nasal cannula directed air into my nostrils through plastic tubes, which were held in place by curved plastic arms that fit behind my ears.

A long hose connected to a stationary oxygen concentrator became like an umbilical cord. And the quietness of our home was replaced by the rhythmic pull and boom of the concentrator. The constant bubbling reminded me of an aquarium.

The oxygen therapist also brought a portable tank on a rolling cart. "You can travel with this," he explained.

I nodded, but plans for leaving home were not on my agenda. I felt like a creature from outer space!

After the therapist left, I sat on the sofa, all hooked up. Gloom replaced my normal optimism. I felt embarrassed, lonely, anxious, and depressed.

Choking down a growing lump in my throat, I tried not to become hysterical. Then turning to my husband, using all the control I could muster, I whined, "Walter, if I have to live like this, I just wish the Lord would go ahead and take me home."

My husband looked directly into my eyes. "Liz, don't ever say that again."

Walter's firm love and tender devotion silenced me. His response comforted me and reassured me of my worth. And God used his supportive spirit to plant a seed of courage.

The following week, my three sisters came to visit. Sarah, a nurse, offered some tips to help me adjust. But I was still embarrassed about my equipment.

On Saturday she suggested, "Why don't we all go to church together in the morning?"

What will people think when they see me? I worried. *Folks will not want to talk with me like they used to.* I resisted, but Sarah didn't give up. Finally I agreed, but only if we'd sit in the back row and leave right after the last "amen."

My family complied, but it was the longest service I'd ever attended. As we were leaving, a woman I'd met two months earlier greeted us. As usual, Kris was friendly and smiling. And much to my surprise, she didn't comment about my equipment. Then she gave me a big hug and promised to be in touch. Attending church had been a challenge, but Kris's warm acceptance paved the way for my return the next Sunday.

Kris followed through by inviting Walter and me to have dinner with her family that week. She put me at ease by focusing on my personality, not my disability. But I still felt anxious about venturing out in other settings. A few weeks after my sisters left, my friend Kay invited me to go shopping.

"Thanks for asking," I told her, "but I can't go."

A few hours later, though, I found myself walking the mall with Kay, dragging my portable oxygen tank and wishing I were invisible. I suggested we spend most of our time at the fabric store, where I hid behind bolts of colorful material. Kay graciously went along with my scheme.

That outing was a milestone. As we were leaving the parking lot, I noticed a man who had no arms. He was smiling. I was stunned. But as I focused on the severity of his disability, I felt ashamed.

"O Lord," I whispered, "how could I be so ungrateful? How could I moan and complain about my disability? Please forgive me."

After Kay took me home, I began to realize that being paralyzed by fear, resentment, and embarrassment did not honor the Creator who gave me life.

The next morning, as I opened my Bible to read a daily devotional, I saw the words, "So do not fear, for I am with you; do not be dismayed, for I am your God. I will strengthen you and help you; I will uphold you with my righteous right hand" (Isaiah 41:10, NIV).

A second verse encouraged me. "Do not grieve, for the joy of the LORD is your strength" (Nehemiah 8:10, NIV).

If the man with no arms could smile, then the Lord could give me strength, too. When I felt afraid, I could remember His presence. Instead of feeling embarrassed, I could think about Him beside me, holding my hand.

I considered the words on a plaque I'd seen: "Lord, help me remember that nothing will happen today that You and I together can't handle." Immediately I began thanking God for the blessing of life, for my loving husband, for my sisters and friends . . . and even for the oxygen tank.

I decided to resist the temptation to isolate myself or mope and instead looked as fresh and glowing as possible and let His joy overflow to others. Nevertheless, I felt awkward the first day I drove myself to the grocery store. When I arrived, I jumped out of the car and slammed the door on my tubing. Though I hoped no one had seen, it did put a smile on my face.

As I stood in the checkout line, wearing my nasal cannula and pulling my tank, a woman approached me. "My brother uses oxygen, but he won't leave home," she said. "How do you manage? We can't seem to motivate him to get out."

"I understand how he must feel," I confessed. "I've been struggling with fear, too. Even so, I decided to be thankful that oxygen is available for me, and I rely on the Lord to be my strength."

We exchanged ideas, and at the close of the conversation she said, "I really admire you." My spirits soared as I loaded my tank in the car and drove home.

A few days later I saw a friend I hadn't seen for some time. She greeted me with, "Look, here comes Miss Sunshine!" An overcoming spirit had gradually replaced my negative attitude and self-pity. These past nine years I've found that through daily prayer and personal application of Scripture, I've been able to change my thinking pattern. I also meditate on great hymns of faith. The less I focus on myself and the more I trust Christ to provide strength each day, the more courageous I feel.

Consequently, the equipment that first immobilized me has opened many doors for witnessing. After a few years, I learned about a new Better Breathing Club. As a veteran oxygen-user, I thought I knew everything on the subject. But God's Spirit kept nudging me to change my mind. Perhaps He wanted me to reach out to someone.

At the first meeting, I met Hilda. She needed a friend. Three days later we had coffee in my home, and I had an opportunity to tell her what Jesus means to me. She wanted to know more. Although she did not pray to receive Christ that day, I continue to nurture our friendship and pray for her daily.

One day I took my empty oxygen tank for a refill. Sam was the technician on duty. After we'd talked a few minutes, he asked, "Mrs. Garland, how do you stay so cheerful?"

That opened the door for me to explain how I find courage and strength through God's Word. I felt a deep satisfaction when he gratefully accepted a small New Testament I'd tucked inside my purse that morning. On a subsequent visit, tears filled my eyes as Sam told me he had received Christ.

Over the years, I have become more comfortable with my apparatus. One day while I was shopping, a curious child yanked on his mother's dress and asked, "What's that, Mommy?"

I approached the boy and his mother and asked, "Would you like to see how this works?" After my brief explanation, the mother was relieved and the boy's curiosity was satisfied. I felt uplifted, too.

Scripture reminds me to not be surprised when troubles come (see James 1:2; 1 Peter 4:12). And I've learned that the way I adapt to trouble is sometimes more important than the trouble itself.

My natural tendency is to withdraw and complain. But when I surrender my feelings to Christ and draw on the security of His power, I am filled with boldness, peace, and joy.

Faithlifter
Joy

IN HER SHOES

Liz found joy, not because of her circumstances, but because she sought a Christlike attitude each day. Can you identify with Liz's initial temptation to withdraw and feel depressed after learning about her need for supplemental oxygen? Have you or someone in your family dealt with a similar experience? How did you handle it? Developing a good sense of humor, as Liz did, will help in all kinds of situations. Are you taking yourself too seriously, or have you discovered the healing qualities of hearty laughter?

A turning point for Liz was seeing a man without arms and realizing that her infirmity was dwarfed by comparison. Not only did she become thankful, but the gladness of her heart put a smile on her face that radiated to all. She also discovered the satisfaction of serving others by sharing with them the joy of her salvation. Has Liz's story stimulated you to be more thankful today?

IN HIS WORD

Happiness often depends on temporal pleasures that may come and go. How is joy different? Does God really want us to be joyful? How can we find joy?

Paul Thigpen wrote, "In the beginning was joy, and the joy was within God, and the joy flowed from God. For the Father eternally loved the Son and the Spirit; and the Son and the Spirit loved the Father and loved each other as well. So the love that holds all things together by its limitless power is the fount of joy, the head of a mighty river that flows in singing superabundance from the heart of God."[1]

God Himself is the source of joy. "You will make known to me the path of life; in Your presence is fullness of joy; in Your right hand there are pleasures forever" (Psalm 16:11).

Words meaning "joy and delight" and "to rejoice" are used numerous times in both the Old and New Testaments. Jesus was a Man of Sorrows but also a Man of Joy. He told His followers, "These things I have spoken to you so that My joy may be in you, and that your joy may be made full" (John 15:11). God wants us to have joy — deep, abiding, radiant, and eternal joy that can be found only through a personal relationship with Him. "There is joy in the presence of the angels of God over one sinner who repents" (Luke 15:10).

"I will rejoice greatly in the Lord, my soul will exult in my God; for He has clothed me with garments of salvation, He has wrapped me with a robe of righteousness, as a bridegroom decks himself with a garland, and as a bride adorns herself with her jewels" (Isaiah 61:10).

God's promise was fulfilled when Christ came. The angel told the shepherds of Bethlehem, "Do not be afraid; for behold, I bring you good news of great joy which shall be for all the people; for today in the city of David there has been born for you a Savior, who is Christ the Lord" (Luke 2:10-11).

Does joy mean we will never be unhappy or suffer? Not at all. The apostle Paul rejoiced in knowing Christ — not only the power of His resurrection, but also the fellowship of His sufferings (see Philippians 3:10). Joy comes in knowing Jesus, who said, "In the world you have tribulation, but take courage; I have overcome the world" (John 16:33).

IN YOUR LIFE
Here are a few suggestions for finding and maintaining joy:

Accept the invitation and come to the party!
Jesus taught in a parable that the kingdom of God is like a wedding feast (see Matthew 22:1-14). You and I are invited. God wants us to have joy, and the first step is receiving Him. I once heard that "joy is the flag that flies when the King is in residence."

Think joyful thoughts.

Instead of letting the joy-robbers of worry, jealousy, or anxiety control your mind, you can obey God with your thoughts: "Whatever is true, whatever is honorable, whatever is right, whatever is pure, whatever is lovely, whatever is of good repute, if there is any excellence and if anything worthy of praise, dwell on these things" (Philippians 4:8).

Affirm your trust in God.

Charles Swindoll wrote, "Joy is a choice. It is a matter of attitude that stems from one's confidence in God—that He is at work, that He is in full control, that He is in the midst of whatever has happened, is happening, and will happen."[2]

Sing joyful songs and praises.

Have you ever lost your song? Or has your heart been so full of joy that you could not keep from singing? Singing praise choruses or hymns to God is a great way to reinforce feelings of joy, regardless of the situation. God listens . . . even to songs in the night.

Anticipate heaven's joy.

We live in enemy territory on earth, and sometimes our joy is hindered by our own sin, but we can look forward to a day when Jesus will make our joy complete. "Therefore you too have grief now; but I will see you again, and your heart will rejoice, and no one will take your joy away from you" (John 16:22).

Remember God's past faithfulness.

One of the antidotes to depression is to recall God's blessings. Often the children of Israel recounted their blessings and restored their joy. If you have lost fellowship with God, cultivating a grateful spirit will remind you of His many blessings, including your salvation.

"Restore to me the joy of Your salvation, and sustain me with a willing spirit" (Psalm 51:12).

"The stronghold of the Christian faith is the joy *of God*, not my joy *in God*. . . . God reigns and rules and rejoices, and His joy is our strength."[3]

A joyful heart is good medicine!

CHAPTER THIRTEEN

Anna, God's Gift

Jeanette Scott

My obstetrician had tears in his eyes as he told me about our new-born daughter. "Jeanette, I'm sorry. There appears to be a problem. Your baby is mentally retarded."

Knowing that our bright, active seven-year-old daughter, Sandy, was normal, my husband, John, and I had never dreamed of having a less-than-perfect baby.

"Are you sure?" I asked. It didn't seem possible.

He explained that Anna had every sign of being a Down's syndrome baby. I still had my doubts, but they were addressed later by the pediatrician, who confirmed the chromosome tests and said, "I am skeptical she can even be potty-trained."

"Will she go to school?" I asked, my voice quivering.

"No, I don't think so," he said thoughtfully, adding, "You'll be lucky if she does."

All I could think about was Dale Evans' book *Angel Unaware*, which described Dale and Roy's grief after the death of their Down's syndrome baby. I thought our baby would die, too. After the doctors explained the situation to John, he came into the room to comfort me. As we held each other and cried together, our dreams dashed, we realized neither of us felt prepared to face the future with our special-needs baby.

Since receiving Christ three years earlier, I had studied God's Word, attended church regularly, and prayed every day. In the quietness of my hospital room, I felt cheated as I yelled out in my heart, *Lord, I've promised to give You the rest of my life, and now this is what You've done!*

Fear paralyzed me as I worried about taking Anna home, wondering if she would be like two handicapped boys I had known who rocked continually. With a negative outlook, I tried to visualize our dreadful future and wondered, *Will Anna be like them?*

Our pastor visited me in the hospital and I felt comforted but also convicted by something he said. "Jeanette," he tenderly asked, "are you willing and prepared to face the ministry God has for you at this time?"

Inwardly, I said, *No! I don't want a ministry. I want a normal, healthy daughter.* But instead of letting my true feelings be known, I put on my best "Christian mask," smiled pleasantly, and through my tears nodded affirmatively.

The arrival of a new baby was supposed to be a happy time, but during the early adjustment period, other family members joined me in weeping. Our older daughter, Sandy, was puzzled about the situation, and one day when John and his mother sat at the kitchen table, Sandy innocently asked, "Why is everyone crying?"

John carefully explained the situation and Sandy accepted it without much emotion. After we brought Anna home and I had more time to talk with Sandy, she really understood. I answered as many of her questions as I could, and Sandy cried for about fifteen minutes. Then she got up and went to play, and from that day, she seemed okay.

My inner conflict continued after we took Anna home. She was not the child I had planned for. However, somehow we made it through the first few days with the support of family and friends.

Anna seemed fine. She was nursing well and didn't have any unusual problems that we could detect. Even though she was quieter and slower than some other babies, we decided to treat her as we would a normal child. The characteristic I noticed most of all was her calm and peaceful spirit. Gradually my heart softened toward her as I cradled her in my arms and viewed her sweet, irreproachable smile. My initial anger began to subside, but disappointment lingered.

Friends from church came every few days to encourage us and help with the chores. John's male friends prayed with him and uplifted him frequently. He and I coped with our grief and loss of expectations in different ways. It was difficult for us to discuss our feelings with each other because they were so opposite. John kept making positive statements about how well Anna was doing, while I wanted to tell him how I *really* felt.

During the first year, our family and friends faithfully prayed for us, and I gained strength as the Lord answered their prayers. One day while grappling with reality, I read a daily devotional that included these healing words from Scripture: "When you pass through the waters, I will be with you; and when you pass through the rivers, they will not sweep over you. When you walk through the fire, you will not be burned; the flames will not set you ablaze. For I am the LORD, your God, the Holy One of Israel, your Savior" (Isaiah 43:2-3, NIV).

Through those verses, the Lord confirmed in my spirit that He would be with me, I would make it, and I would not be overwhelmed. After that day, John and I talked about constructive steps we could take to improve our situation. As a result, we trusted the Lord for the funds and began taking Anna to a nearby child development center. Anna's motor skills improved, and she began walking at thirteen months. Amazing! We were even more thrilled when she was potty-trained at four years. Truly I could see God's graciousness as we prayed through each physical hurdle.

The medical staff marveled at her progress as she eventually learned to dress herself, brush her teeth, and generally take care of her basic needs. Fortunately, our parents lived nearby and developed a close relationship with both the girls. Periodically they stayed with the children overnight so John and I could take short trips. The Lord provided those wonderful grandparents "for such a time as this."

Anna's progress continued to the point she was able to attend a local private school from age three through five, and then she began public school. Her cheerful disposition and irrepressible smiles endeared her to me and to others as well.

Her abilities continued to amaze us. I taught piano lessons in our home after school, and apparently Anna had been listening carefully to the music. One day after a student had been playing "Noel," we were shocked when Anna later sat at the piano and began playing the same piece by ear. Then she played "Holy, Holy, Holy." Her musical talent reminds us of our heavenly Father's creativity, and as she plays, she expresses love for Him.

Anna received Christ while attending a special class for mentally and physically handicapped people at a local church. She has simple faith. When someone in her class died, she said, "He wasn't at school."

I said, "He went to be with Jesus."

She added, "He is in heaven."

Although our doctors warned us that Anna would probably not learn to read, we worked with her at home. When we asked her teachers to try to overcome the obstacle, some were skeptical; but now Anna reads on a third-grade level, and she has a wonderful memory. Teachers in the lower grades taught her the presidents of the United States, and Anna still remembers all of them and quotes the full names!

When she went through puberty and began menses at age nine, I had trouble convincing her to wear a pad during her period. Finally John said, "Let me talk with her."

"Anna," he said while making eye contact, "if you wear the pad, you will get well." Anna nodded her head. She understood and obeyed her dad with no further difficulty.

One time she needed to take oral antibiotics but couldn't swallow a pill. John showed her how to put the pill on the back of her tongue and swallow it. After she gulped down the pill, we clapped. Down's syndrome children love praise. If we ever forgot to clap for her after she ingested a pill, she tugged on John's arm as a reminder.

We have taught Anna to have good manners, and she usually behaves well when we go to public places. At first we questioned the decision to take her with us to Disney World, but she did great and thoroughly enjoyed it. Anna prefers one-on-one relationships, but dislikes fussing, children crying, or loud talking. Those things frustrate her because she doesn't know how to handle them.

When Anna was twenty-four, she began having unexplained mood swings and emotional outbursts that we were unable to correct with medication or any other resources. Our stress level was at the breaking point, and it became more difficult for our married daughter, Sandy, and her family to visit us because of Anna's agitation around our grandchildren.

One day when the situation seemed hopeless, I thought, *I have a choice to make. I can either let this overwhelm me or I can trust the Lord.* Within an hour after praying, the Lord impressed a verse upon my spirit: "Do not be afraid or discouraged because of this vast army. For the battle is not yours, but God's" (2 Chronicles 20:15, NIV). At that moment, I sensed great peace, and God began to work in ways I could not imagine.

We had never considered a group home as an option for Anna until then, but God led us on a diligent search, and after visiting a number of facilities, we placed Anna in a group home in our hometown. It has worked out beautifully. At age twenty-seven, Anna is currently thriving there and becoming more independent each day, and we enjoy visiting her and seeing her at church. God did not give us a handicapped child without giving us the love, wisdom, and resources to care for her, and I believe He led us to place her in the group home as an extension of that loving care. It has been a blessing for all.

Since Anna was born into our family, I have learned so much that now I can truly thank God for the trials He has seen us through. He met our every need, whether it was financial or emotional.

Though I still do not understand why Anna was born with Down's syndrome, I stopped blaming God long ago. In fact, I now realize Anna was not an *accident*; she is unique because of the way He made her. The Lord really got my attention one day through His Word: "Did not he who made me in the womb make them? Did not the same one form us both within our mothers?" (Job 31:15, NIV).

I confess that it took a long time for me to see Anna as God's gift, to value her in that way, and to arrive at peaceful acceptance. However, her extra-precious smile and childlike faith still remind me that God is in control, and no matter what happens, we can trust Him.

Faithlifter
Truth

IN HER SHOES

Jeanette transparently described her initial feelings about Anna. Because of her disappointment, it took Jeanette a long time to see her daughter in a different light. Have you ever had a situation in which your shock and disappointment caused you to be very angry? Have you ever felt that God really let you down? Where did you turn for encouragement?

I asked Jeanette if she could refer to any books that had helped her along the way. And she answered simply, "My help was from the Bible, God's Word." The Lord's Spirit always led Jeanette to the verses she needed. When your expectations fall short, can you, too, rely on God's truth to bring encouragement and hope?

IN HIS WORD

The Greek word for *truth* means "sincerity, conformity with established facts, accuracy, and reality based upon the essence of a matter." Here are some insights about truth:

Biblical truth is based on the person of God Himself.
"I will proclaim the name of the LORD. Oh, praise the greatness of our God! He is the Rock, his works are perfect, and all his ways are just. A faithful God who does no wrong, upright and just is he" (Deuteronomy 32:3-4, NIV).

"Into your hands I commit my spirit; redeem me, O LORD, the God of truth" (Psalm 31:5, NIV).

Truth also describes God's Son, Jesus.
"The Word became flesh and made his dwelling among us. We have seen his glory, the glory of the One and Only, who came

from the Father, full of grace and truth" (John 1:14, NIV).

"Jesus answered, 'I am the way and the truth and the life. No one comes to the Father except through me. If you really knew me, you would know my Father as well. From now on, you do know him and have seen him'" (John 14:6-7, NIV).

Truth is God's Word.

"Sanctify them by the truth; your word is truth" (John 17:17, NIV).

"True instruction was in his mouth and nothing false was found on his lips. He walked with me in peace and uprightness, and turned many from sin" (Malachi 2:6, NIV).

"Do your best to present yourself to God as one approved, a workman who does not need to be ashamed and who correctly handles the word of truth" (2 Timothy 2:15, NIV).

In Your Life

Oswald Chambers wrote, "The life of faith is not a life of mounting up with wings, but a life of walking and not fainting."[1] How can we establish a strong faith that will weather the storm?

Base your faith upon fact, not feelings.

Many Scriptures teach this truth, but this one always touches my heart: "Are not two sparrows sold for a penny? Yet not one of them will fall to the ground apart from the will of your Father. And even the very hairs of your head are all numbered. So don't be afraid; you are worth more than many sparrows" (Matthew 10:29-31, NIV).

One of my favorite hymns is "His Eye Is on the Sparrow" because it reminds me that if God takes care of the sparrow, He will surely take care of me, too.

Remember that God takes care of His own.

"Many are the woes of the wicked, but the LORD's unfailing love surrounds the man who trusts in him" (Psalm 32:10, NIV). This is good to know because when we are in a painful situation, we do not always feel that God loves us. However, often the way God's love is manifested is through His faithful children becoming His hands and feet, ministering and showing love.

Don't forget in the dark what you learned in the light.

I once heard Dr. Joseph Bayly, who had experienced the death of three children, say, "Never forget in the dark what you have learned in the light."

God never intended us to know everything, but He will reveal to us all we need to know. If we knew and understood everything, we'd have no need for faith. In our own minds and hearts, God would be diminished. Some things we're not able to understand anyway, and some things are best left unknown. So in His time, God may disclose some things to us, but in some instances, His love gift may be silence. The most important thing to remember is that we never walk alone. He has promised, "I will never desert you, nor will I ever forsake you" (Hebrews 13:5).

David expressed his childlike trust in the wisdom of God when he wrote: "O LORD, my heart is not proud, nor my eyes haughty; nor do I involve myself in great matters, or in things too difficult for me. Surely I have composed and quieted my soul; like a weaned child rests against his mother, my soul is like a weaned child within me" (Psalm 131:1-2).

Author Jerry Bridges adds: "If we are to honor God by trusting Him, and if we are to find peace for ourselves, we must come to the place where we can honestly say, 'God, I do not have to understand. I will just trust You.'"[2]

Apply the Word in your life.

Here are some practical suggestions for getting started:

- Define a problem in your own life (anger, jealousy, worry, inability to forgive).

- Use a concordance and look up verses related to that subject.
- Write out Scripture verses on 3 x 5 cards and place them where you can meditate on their meaning (above the kitchen sink, by your makeup mirror, on the dashboard of the car).
- Think about what a particular verse is saying to you and how you might change your actions or reactions to line up with its teaching.
- Write insights as they occur to you.
- Dig deeper. Use commentaries and other Bible study helps to elaborate on the meaning.
- Try writing out your own paraphrase from a passage.
- Start your day by reading a devotional each morning that includes Scripture.
- Choose a plan for reading through the Bible in a year.

CHAPTER FOURTEEN

Help! My Husband Lost His Job

Lana Key[*]

For months we had been planning our ten-day vacation, a special getaway to New England in the spring. My husband had worked as an accountant for a Christian organization for more than thirteen years, and I was employed as a registered nurse in a local hospital. We had always been careful with our finances and had saved and planned diligently for a much-needed vacation.

The day before we were to leave on our prepaid trip, David came home and announced, "My job is being eliminated."

"What do you mean?" I asked in disbelief. Although David was normally serious-minded, I thought surely this wasn't for real.

"The organization has been restructured, and my position has been eliminated." He paused, took a deep breath, and added, "I just found out today." David's voice trailed into silence as I tried to cope with the meaning of it all. He wasn't kidding.

At first I felt angry. David had been such a loyal employee and had gone the extra mile many times. He was dependable, efficient,

[*]Lana Key is a pseudonym

and experienced, and to think that his skills were not appreciated discouraged me greatly and at the same time sparked a fury of anger within. My next reaction was to share David's disappointment, with many tears. Together we grieved. It was like a death. The timing couldn't have been worse. Not only were we planning our trip, but we had promised to fund the educations of both our college-age daughters.

Suddenly I felt scared, knowing that alone I would be supporting our family. My nursing position seemed secure, but with budget cutbacks, part of the nursing staff was dismissed on some "low census" days. With overtime pay being eliminated, I knew I'd be fortunate just to get a regular paycheck. The financial security we had enjoyed to that point vanished. I felt anxious as well, not knowing how long it would take David to find employment and what major lifestyle changes we might be required to make.

"What are we going to do?" I wondered aloud.

David put his arm around me and said, "Lana, we need this vacation. We've planned for it, paid for it, and I think we should go. We'll just pray and I'll start searching for another job when we get back."

Our vacation travel went well, the scenery was spectacular and the weather was lovely—but I cried a lot. The loss of David's job had put a damper on an otherwise beautiful trip, even though we tried not to dwell on it. After we returned, David began searching for employment. He scanned the Sunday paper want ads and sent out six to ten résumés weekly. Sadly, none developed into prospects.

One morning my devotional reading included Psalm 37:25: "I was young and now I am old, yet I have never seen the righteous forsaken or their children begging bread" (NIV). I thought, *That's good. At least the Lord says we won't go hungry.*

Finally, David received an encouraging inquiry, but as he traveled across town to his appointment, an aggressive driver ran him off the road, causing him to totally wreck the newer of our two cars. Fortunately, David was not injured, but I was upset that we had to borrow a family member's car and, eventually, buy another used car for transportation. Although David rented a car and actually reached the interview, it turned out to be yet another false hope.

During the course of the next twenty-four months, three solid prospects did not materialize. We would become excited and willing to move out of state, if necessary, but when the painful negative responses came, we felt taunted—as if we had reached for a treasure but the treasure chest was empty.

We managed by cutting back on all nonessential items and adhering to a strict budget. I took extra "call" at the hospital and worked overtime when possible. The added burden of being the sole provider caused me to become very health-conscious, thinking, *I have to stay well and not do anything foolish that would keep me from working.* I was always careful anyway, but just the possibility of sustaining an injury after exercising caused me to cringe. Even when driving, my heart fluttered as I prayed, "O Lord, please don't let me have an accident."

David and I were careful not to say things that would hurt each other, but we seldom had fun, and our relationship suffered. Although our marriage was not actually in danger of disintegrating, many times we failed to be supportive, and our communication became superficial and shallow. We continued with regular but sometimes perfunctory church attendance, and we tithed faithfully, but our giving did not always match "the cheerful giver" described in Scripture.

After the first year of waiting for permanent employment, David and I found comfort in talking with our pastor and his wife, who had years earlier survived a similar experience. A hospital coworker whose husband had also been without work for an extended period of time told me about some of her frustrations and adjustments. Hearing about others' similar trials really helped.

Outwardly, I tried to reassure David: "David, you are a capable accountant, and this time without a job is not a reflection upon you personally; it mostly reflects the economic conditions." Even though I had no idea about the future, I heard myself add, "I know that somehow God will open a door."

Inwardly, however, on my lowest days I could not help but talk with God about my own feelings. In lengthy self-examinations I wondered, *Lord, what have I done to cause this? Is this situation happening because of some sin in my past?* As a young couple, we had lost two infants, and I would sometimes think, *Lord, where were You then and where are You now? Do You really care?* Negative thoughts bred more negative thoughts, and the negative spiral sent my emotions twirling downward.

On the other hand, my husband's faith was always strong, and sometimes I would get irritated when it seemed he was not being aggressive enough or realistic enough about our situation. Looking back on some days, I was about as supportive as Job's wife (Remember? She is the one who spouted discouraging phrases like "curse God and die"), but I kept those words and thoughts to myself.

My greatest solace was my sister, Jan. She would say and do things to brighten my spirits. I could express my negative feelings and pain with her and not have to hurt David. So many times we sat together sipping tea on her front porch swing while she listened with an understanding heart and a nonjudgmental attitude. When my prayer life was at a low ebb, she would pray with me and for me. She sent cards and Scriptures and asked several of her friends to do the same. Knowing that her Sunday school class prayed for us really helped.

David had taken a temporary full-time job that provided some income, so we rocked along in a "make-do" or "maybe-it-won't-get-any-better" mode. My patience wore thin; I despised the waiting room.

My Bible was almost worn out on the page containing Philippians 4:6-7: "Don't worry about anything; instead, pray about everything; tell God your needs, and don't forget to thank him for his answers. If you do this you will experience God's peace, which is far more wonderful than the human mind can understand. His peace will keep your thoughts and your hearts quiet and at rest as you trust in Christ Jesus" (TLB).

Finally, just when I had almost given up, a Christian organization in Arkansas contacted David regarding a current job opening, an opportunity we knew nothing about. I watched with utter amazement as God orchestrated all the events. We traveled to Arkansas for the interview and found the situation impressive. David seemed perfect for the job, and they were thrilled with his expertise. A few days later they called and made an offer.

Within weeks, we sold our house and purchased a home in Arkansas. I found a nursing management position almost identical to my former one. We visited a church that we really liked and quickly began cultivating new friendships. I felt so excited and light-hearted, freed from the mantle of gloom that had surrounded our family for the past two and a half years. God had opened a new and very special door we did not even know existed, but He knew what was best for us all along, and the timing was perfect.

Looking back, I feel sad that my faith seemed so weak and inse-cure at times. But I had continued to give, pray, read the Bible, and attend church, even when I hadn't felt like it. We had much to be thankful for. Our two daughters were frugal, supportive, helpful, and very understanding during our distress. Somehow we even man-aged to fund our younger daughter's wedding just before the move.

I thought of how I once had little compassion for others who were in jobless situations—but that changed. Unfortunately, I had often looked on the negative side of things instead of counting our blessings. As I stopped to thank God for what He had done, I real-ized *He was there all the time* through our supportive friends, one of whom had helped David find his interim work. God provided for all of our needs. Our want list was severely shortened, but we were able to pay all our bills on time, and although some repairs had to be delayed, most were eventually done. My job had provided our health insurance, and fortunately we did not have any major illnesses. Our situation could have been so much worse!

As David nears retirement age, we recall that frightful time and thank God for His abundant provision. Though I would not want to go through it again, our trial of extended financial insecurity taught me many lessons, including patience. Three things I now know: God knows best, He is in control, and He cares deeply about what happens to each one of us.

Faithlifter
Patience

IN HER SHOES

Lana and her husband traversed the troubled waters of his unemployment, but they managed to stay together and learn from their trials. Have you ever had a similar experience? Lana candidly shared her feelings and frustrations, yet she and David exercised diligent stewardship in managing the funds they had. She learned a lesson in compassion toward others in similar circumstances and also discovered that she and David were not alone. How did she relate to her husband in his time of need?

What temptations would someone in Lana's position face? As a result of this testing time she changed her way of thinking. What did she learn? Her vulnerability in sharing this story is an indication of her love for the Lord and her desire to encourage others.

IN HIS WORD

Patience is one of the hallmarks of Christlike character, but it is one of the most difficult qualities to apply in our own lives. Here are some Scriptures to help us understand why:

Trials and patience go hand in hand.

"Consider it all joy, my brethren, when you encounter various trials, knowing that the testing of your faith produces endurance. And let endurance have its perfect result, so that you may be perfect and complete, lacking in nothing" (James 1:2-4).

Christ is our example.

In these verses, the writer of Hebrews refers to the patience of Christ and our fellowship with Him: "Therefore, since we have so great a cloud of witnesses surrounding us, let us also lay aside every encumbrance and the sin which so easily entangles us, and let us run with endurance the race that is set before us, fixing our eyes on Jesus, the author and perfecter of faith, who for the joy set before Him endured the cross, despising the shame, and has sat down at the right hand of the throne of God" (Hebrews 12:1-2).

The apostle Paul encouraged new Christians to have patience.
"Now you followed my teaching, conduct, purpose, faith, patience, love, perseverance, persecutions, and sufferings, such as happened to me at Antioch, at Iconium and at Lystra; what persecutions I endured, and out of them all the Lord rescued me!" (2 Timothy 3:10-11).

Paul prayed for the church in Colosse that the saints there would be "strengthened with all power, according to His glorious might, for the attaining of all steadfastness and patience" (Colossians 1:11).

He also prayed for the Ephesians believers "that He would grant you, according to the riches of His glory, to be strengthened with power through His Spirit in the inner man" (Ephesians 3:16).

Patience has its rewards.
Patience during undeserved affliction brings God's favor. "For what credit is there if, when you sin and are harshly treated, you endure it with patience? But if when you do what is right and suffer for it you patiently endure it, this finds favor with God" (1 Peter 2:20).

"And we desire that each one of you show the same diligence so as to realize the full assurance of hope until the end, so that you may not be sluggish, but imitators of those who through faith and patience inherit the promises" (Hebrews 6:11-12).

"Therefore be patient, brethren, until the coming of the Lord. The farmer waits for the precious produce of the soil, being patient about it, until it gets the early and late rains. You too be patient; strengthen your hearts, for the coming of the Lord is near" (James 5:7-8).

In Your Life

In his book *God Isn't in a Hurry*, Warren Wiersbe suggests, "When we find ourselves in a difficult situation, most of us pray, 'Father, get me out of this!' If nothing happens immediately, then we pray, 'Father, *when* will I get out of this?' But what we ought to be praying is, 'Father, what should I get out of this?' There is purpose in trials, and even discouraging days can be excellent teachers of spiritual lessons that we could learn no other way."[1]

Our daughter is teaching our granddaughters, Emily (age four) and Julie (age two), that patience means "waiting with a happy spirit." It is also defined as "calm endurance without complaining." You've likely seen the humorous bumper sticker "Lord, give me patience, and give it to me right now!" Isn't that the way most of us feel? Some of us recall waiting while our food warmed on the stove, but now we impatiently stand at the microwave for a few seconds while tapping our fingers and shifting our weight from one foot to the other. Our culture has programmed us to want everything *now*.

We also find it difficult to wait in life's serious situations when, like the psalmist, we cry out, "How long, O LORD? Will You forget me forever? How long will You hide Your face from me?" (Psalm 13:1). We forget that God may be teaching us forbearance as we wait for Him to act. Here are a few thoughts about waiting:

Waiting encourages persistent prayer.

Sometimes being still and quiet is one of the hardest disciplines of the Christian life. We mothers are great at wanting to jump in and fix every problem that arises in our families. Yet it is better to pray than to do something that we might later regret. Sometimes we learn this the hard way. Prayer is being actively involved in the problem, whatever it is, and trusting God to work things out behind the scenes.

A little sign in my home announces, "There is one God and you are not Him." My children have reminded me about it from time to time when situations have been impossible for me to alter. I confess I'm trying hard to wait, but sometimes it's not easy.

Waiting helps us develop empathy.

When we are forced to wait on the Lord, we quickly find that others have been or are in similar places. If everything happened just as we wanted it to, we would not have the opportunity to look beyond our own selfish interests. Touched with the hurts of others, our ability to relate to them is more sharply defined. When God does meet our need, we are in a position to encourage someone else and tell that person how He came through for us.

Waiting enlarges our dependence on God.

God knows what He is doing. We can either be restless or we can wait with grace, knowing and believing that God sees the bigger picture and His timing is always right. When we praise God and thank Him for what He is going to do before it comes to pass, we put our faith into action and confess our dependence.

Charles Haddon Spurgeon wrote about James 5:11: "Ye have heard of the patience of Job. Did Job learn patience among his flocks or with his camels or with his children when they were feasting? No, he learned it when he sat among the ashes, and scraped himself with a potsherd, and his heart was heavy because of the death of his children. Patience is a pearl which is found only in the deep seas of affliction, and only grace can find it there, bring it to the surface, and adorn the neck of faith with it."[2]

CHAPTER FIFTEEN

Is God Punishing Me?

Fran Caffey Sandin

The house was quiet. The children were asleep and Jim was at work. I sat alone at the kitchen table, plagued with questions that had crossed my mind for several weeks. If I had called the doctor sooner, would Jeffrey have lived? The week before he became ill I had taken Jeffrey with me while running some errands. If only I had left him at home, would he have escaped the seemingly inexplicable illness? While pondering and searching for answers, I wondered again and again if our toddler-son's death was due to God's disapproval of something I had done.

Perhaps God was chastening me for some foolish remark. Once while chatting with my sister I said flippantly, "I was so surprised when Jeffrey was born. Instead of a boy I was expecting a dark-haired, brown-eyed girl." As I reflected upon this conversation, I wondered if God was unhappy with me for making that comment. Had I seemed ungrateful for our son? Surely not. Jeffrey was a beautiful, blond-haired, blue-eyed, healthy baby, and I loved him deeply.

Maybe God was correcting me for my failures as a mother. I knew I had made mistakes. While I had never knowingly or intentionally harmed the children, occasionally I had reacted with anger and impatience.

I reflected on one day in particular when exhaustion compelled me to take an afternoon nap. Our three preschoolers were tucked into their beds, too; but just as I completely relaxed and closed my eyes, Steve and Jeffrey began making noises. They were getting in and out of bed in spite of my instructions to the contrary.

Exasperated, I grabbed the "rod of correction" and, on short notice, paddled them both. Recalling that event, I thought about the surprised look on Jeffrey's face as big tears rolled down his cheeks. He had cried and cried. Had I overreacted?

I had to remind myself that God instructs us as parents to discipline our children. Even if I failed in some way that day, the ultimate goal was to teach obedience. Surely God knew my heart.

After a time of silent meditation there at the kitchen table, I looked up and caught a glimpse of a booklet on the counter. I reached over, opened it, and began reading *Death of a Little Child*, by J. Vernon McGee. This paragraph comforted me:

> Perhaps you are rebuking yourself for not having done something more in behalf of the child. You may be harassed by a haunting fear that you did something wrong. Martha and Mary felt that the death of their brother could have been averted. They both said to Him, "Lord, if You had been here, my brother would not have died" (John 11:21, 32). Yet in the providence of God it was best for Lazarus to die, though it could have been averted—but only with divine help. Humanly speaking, you did the best that you could, and you must leave the results to Him. Do not reproach yourself for negligence or ignorance. Regardless of what you had done, you are still a fallible and feeble creature. You did the best you could.[1]

The words reassured me, but still I was not satisfied. A new door of nagging doubt opened. I began to recall sins of my past. Like a television rerun they paraded across my mind, and the remembrance was painful. Could it be that Jeffrey's death was God's punishment for my past sins?

A few weeks later, as I attended a Bible study, I was amazed to read that a woman in Scripture had asked the same question. In 1 Kings 17:18, a widow cried to the prophet, asking, "O man of God . . . what have you done to me? Have you come here to punish my sins by killing my son?" (TLB). This woman's poignant cry revealed her acute awareness of sin. I identified with her.

However, within minutes a different thought emerged. Even though I felt a sense of shame for my sins, I knew I had prayed and asked forgiveness according to 1 John 1:9: "If we confess our sins, He is faithful and righteous to forgive us our sins and to cleanse us from all unrighteousness." I began to realize that if God had forgiven me, I must forgive myself. Otherwise I would not be acting on God's personal word to me.

Divine guidance seemed at work a couple of days later when my dear friend Linda brought me a magazine that featured the following verses in bold type, occupying an entire page of the publication:

The LORD is merciful and gracious, slow to anger, and plenteous in mercy. He will not always chide: neither will he keep his anger for ever. He hath not dealt with us after our sins; nor rewarded us according to our iniquities. For as the heaven is high above the earth, so great is his mercy toward them that fear him. As far as the east is from the west, so far hath he removed our transgressions from us. Like as a father pitieth his children, so the LORD pitieth them that fear him. For he knoweth our frame; he remembereth that we are dust. (Psalm 103:8-14, KJV)

For a time, it was difficult for me to feel forgiven, though I knew it was true. I even began thinking of small regrets—things I wished

I had done for Jeffrey, like having a professional photograph made of just him.

In His tender way, the Lord addressed my concerns through the pages of a book about grief. The author observed that often after the death of a loved one we pile up a huge stack of regrets. We remember what we did that we should not have done; we reconstruct everything we wish we had done. Our heartache intensifies as we suffer through remorseful feelings and guilt. We relive old conflicts if there were any. Responding to these natural tendencies, the author concluded that true healing comes when we accept God's forgiveness and throw away the burden of regret.[2]

Our heavenly Father had graciously reassured my questioning heart concerning foolish remarks, failures as a mother, past sins, and regrets, but He seemed to know how much I needed one final word of encouragement.

It came one Sunday evening as my husband and I listened to a visiting pastor in our local church. As part of his message, he said, "No pain or sorrow that comes to us could be severe enough to punish us for our sins. Sin [falling short of God's moral standards] is so contrary to God that it required the blood of Jesus Christ, His Son, perfect and blameless, to cover the sin of all mankind—once and for all. We must confess our sins and accept His forgiveness."

Continuing, he added, "If we receive Christ into our hearts, accept His forgiveness, and become God's child, then nothing can happen to us that He does not allow. God is interested in how we react to our trials. If we hand Him the pieces of our broken hearts and broken lives, He can take them and make them beautiful."

At that moment I could think of nothing more devastating than Jeffrey's death, and no one more precious than my Lord and Savior, Jesus Christ. I know that in order to get on with normal, healthy living I must leave everything in His forgiving hands and trust Him for tomorrow.

"Is God punishing me?" was a question I could not talk about with anyone except God, but He is the best counselor I know. It took a number of months for me to work through the self-condemnation

I experienced after Jeffrey's illness and death. Through the truth I found in God's Word and the messengers He sent, I learned to leave the questioning behind.

God is faithful. He does make all things beautiful . . . in His time. Assured of His love, mercy, and forgiveness, I began searching for the productive life He designed just for me.

Faithlifter
Mercy

IN HER SHOES

This story is taken from *See You Later, Jeffrey*,[3] a book I wrote following the death of our son. Several readers had commented about how they identified with my feelings. God's mercy has been evident not only in my writing that first little book, but also in opening a door for me to share the stories of other women in this book.

Have you ever, like me, struggled with feelings of condemnation over your failures? How has God encouraged you during a similar time? Only the mercies of God will see us through our struggles with self-doubt or reproach. In what ways have you experienced the mercies of God?

IN HIS WORD

Mercy is one of the attributes of God. "But God, being rich in mercy, because of His great love with which He loved us, even when we were dead in our transgressions, made us alive together with Christ (by grace you have been saved)" (Ephesians 2:4-5).

The Greek word for *mercy* means "the outward manifestation of pity." It assumes the one who receives it has a need, and the one who shows it has adequate resources to meet that need. Grace is God's attitude toward the lawbreaker and the rebel, while mercy is His attitude toward those who are suffering and in distress. He reaches out in compassion, especially when we are helpless. Even after Adam fell into sin and spurned the kindness of God, God remained faithful and provided a way to restore fellowship.

He still reaches out in mercy today. Not only does God look upon the sinner with pity, He deals with the source of our misery — sin. The cross of Christ is the supreme example of God's mercy and saving compassion. "The LORD is gracious and compassionate, slow to anger and rich in love. The LORD is good to all; he has compassion on all he has made" (Psalm 145:8-9, NIV).

Mercy follows grace.

In salvation, the word *grace* precedes the word *mercy*. "To Timothy, my true child in the faith: Grace, mercy and peace from God the Father and Christ Jesus our Lord" (1 Timothy 1:2). When God acts with mercy, the result is manifested as peace in the heart of man. When we're forgiven by His grace, we are blessed by God's mercy and experience the blessing of His peace. "Grace, mercy and peace will be with us, from God the Father and from Jesus Christ, the Son of the Father, in truth and love" (2 John 1:3).

Mercy is found through prayer.

"Therefore let us draw near with confidence to the throne of grace, so that we may receive mercy and find grace to help in time of need" (Hebrews 4:16).

One manifestation of Christ's mercy is that He prays for us. We can come before Him with our requests and know that He will give His timely gift of mercy. It will arrive just at the moment of need.

Mercy involves forgiveness.

"Be kind and compassionate to one another, forgiving each other, just as in Christ God forgave you" (Ephesians 4:32, NIV). When we realize the extent to which Christ has forgiven us and see our sins in the same light that God sees them, it is easier for us to readily forgive others. We, too, have been forgiven a great debt. Just as Christ demonstrated forgiveness and reconciliation toward us, so we are to extend that same mercy toward others.

God's mercy equips us to help others.

"Blessed be the God and Father of our Lord Jesus Christ, the Father of mercies and God of all comfort, who comforts us in all our affliction so that we may be able to comfort those who are in any affliction with the comfort with which we ourselves are comforted by God" (2 Corinthians 1:3-4).

IN YOUR LIFE

Because mercy is from God and we are to imitate Him, how can we show mercy? Here are some thoughts and suggestions:

Deliberately identify with another person's needs.

This means we get into another person's skin so that we think with her mind, feel with her feelings, see with her eyes, and then do something to help alleviate her need. It is easy to become judgmental about another person until we put ourselves in her place.

However, it is good to understand that mercy should be tempered for the good of the individual. Can mercy run amuck? Yes! Justice can be coldhearted at times, and mercy can be seen as lacking resolve. However, mercy looks beyond the moment toward the long-range goal.

For example, parents have to strike the balance in disciplining their children. We see how often God balanced justice and mercy as He dealt with the Israelites in the Old Testament. He forgave them repeatedly, but He also exhibited justice. He did not tolerate their proud and unrepentant hearts, but desired that they walk in humble obedience. Even Jonah had to learn the hard way! Sometimes we do, too.

Choose to extend mercy.

It might be as simple as withholding angry words when someone has verbally wounded you. Does that person deserve retaliation? Probably. But extending mercy is a choice.

Jesus taught, "Blessed are the merciful: for they shall obtain mercy" (Matthew 5:7, KJV). When the Holy Spirit of God lives within us, we can practice mercy in many ways. It can take the form of encouragement through meeting practical needs, sending cards, or even giving a smile or a hug. The parable of the Good Samaritan is an excellent example of showing mercy (see Luke 10:30-37). When a man fell into the hands of robbers, the men beat him and left him half dead along the roadside. Two Jewish religious leaders— a priest and a Levite—passed by on the other side, not wanting to be bothered. But a Samaritan (the Jews looked down on the Samaritans for their religious beliefs) took pity on the robbery victim, bandaged his wounds, poured on oil and wine, and then put the man on his own donkey and took him to an inn, where he paid the innkeeper to take care of him.

After Jesus told this story, He asked, " 'Which of these three do you think was a neighbor to the man who fell into the hands of robbers?' The expert in the law replied, 'The one who had mercy on him.' Jesus told him, 'Go and do likewise' " (Luke 10:36-37, NIV).

When we are battered by life's storms, it helps when someone rubs our bruised egos with the balm of soothing words, prepares a cup of tea, or simply listens and wipes away our tears. After we have experienced God's mercy firsthand, we are more equipped to extend mercy to others as the Holy Spirit leads.

Those who have grieved a particular loss—divorce, a loved one's death, a debilitating injury—have greater compassion for others going through similar trials. They remember what helped them and they are willing to assist. That is mercy received and mercy given, just as Jesus said.

Here are a few guidelines for showing mercy:

- Give mercy prudently and with prayerful discernment. Some situations call for "tough love," and if you continue showing open-ended mercy, the object of your mercy may be relieved of certain pressures the Lord is bringing to make that person accountable.
- Look beyond the faults of others to see their real need.
- Do not expect anything in return. "Give generously to him and do so without a grudging heart; then because of this the

LORD your God will bless you in all your work and in everything you put your hand to" (Deuteronomy 15:10, NIV).

- Extend mercy through Christ and in humility, not for recognition. "He has showed you, O man, what is good. And what does the LORD require of you? To act justly and to love mercy and to walk humbly with your God" (Micah 6:8, NIV).

CHAPTER SIXTEEN

Good-Bye Locusts

Amy Keller[*]

It never occurred to me that our marriage might be in trouble. Throughout our eighteen years together, Bill and I had participated in church activities, taught Sunday school, and led in various capacities. We desired the best for our three children, and to any outsider we appeared to be "the perfect family." Then something happened.

"Amy," Bill said quietly one day, "I have a serious attraction for Martha. Nothing has happened between us, but I just wanted to let you know."

Martha and John were friends from church, and we had gone out to eat together several times. Now I felt sick, like a blow had been delivered to the pit of my stomach, like the wind had been knocked out of my lungs. I didn't know what to say, but finally choked out the words, "Bill, what have I done? I didn't realize you were so unhappy." Later in our conversation, I asked, "Would it help to see a counselor?"

"No," he said confidently, "I think the Holy Spirit will help us work this out."

Amy Keller is a pseudonym

I thought, *Of course, He will help us. We are Christians.* Bill and I discussed a lot of issues that spring, but, unfortunately, we could not sort out the answers.

That summer was difficult for me because we continued to see Martha and John at church, and Bill and I pretended everything was fine. When my concern overwhelmed me, I would try to talk with Bill about my feelings, but he said, "Just stay busy and don't talk about it. Everything will be okay."

Bill had a melancholy temperament and that worked for him, but I was a talkative, outgoing sanguine, and I felt like a pressure cooker about to explode. My mind raced ahead of the situation as my imagination took over. Finally, one day during extended prayer, several Scriptures came to mind, including the verses that explain how God hates divorce (see Malachi 2:14-16). I responded by saying, "Lord, if You hate divorce, then I claim that divorce is not Your will for us, and somehow You will help us work things out and stay together."

School began. In the busy routine, I mentally placed the entire situation on the back burner and gradually started feeling better and thinking perhaps our marriage relationship was improving and moving forward. Unfortunately, that was not the case. One fall morning after Bill left for work, I decided to drive to his office, only to discover that he had not shown up for work and no one knew his whereabouts. He had left us.

Bill had written farewell letters addressed to the children and to me and placed them in plain sight on his desk. I was devastated. What would I do? How would I break the news to the children? He was a wonderful dad whom they loved very much. How could this be happening to a Christian family who claimed they were "living for the Lord"? I had no idea where Bill had gone and if I would ever see him again.

I picked up the phone on Bill's desk and called our pastor, and after I told him the situation, he said, "Amy, don't worry. I think I can help. I'll get back in touch with you after I make a few calls."

Within a few minutes he called back to say that Martha was also missing, and he would be back in touch after investigating the situation further.

Suspended between a state of shock and the reality of having both my pride and my security stripped away, I drove home and wept uncontrollably. Between sobs, I cried out, "Oh, God, please help me! I don't know what to do."

Several Scriptures came alive, fresh and new in my mind, and I could actually visualize the Lord's extended hand filled with manna as He said, "Take. Eat. I will take care of you." I felt the breath of His presence and the mantle of His grace and peace covering me like a soft down comforter. He spoke to my heart in ways I cannot explain.

Painful though it was, agonizing days of waiting stimulated serious soul-searching, and I pondered, *How have I contributed to our crumbling marriage?* Over a period of several days, the painful answers unfolded. Busyness with the children had distracted me from focusing on my husband's need for my undivided attention, encouraging words, and time set apart for intimacy. Gradual preoccupation with other things—good things, but not God's best—had caused unintentional neglect. I thought I knew how to be a good wife, but the truth I now saw was not pretty.

It also became clear that I had previously placed my security in Bill instead of in the Lord. Only later would I understand more about God's sovereignty and that I could not control the current situation, only my response to it. My faith began to grow when I trusted in Him alone.

Our pastor and I were in touch by phone several times, and at one point he counseled me to read Jeremiah 18:1-6. "Amy, put your name in place of 'Israel' and realize that, like a vessel that has been broken, your marriage is also broken. But if you allow God to put you back on the potter's wheel, your marriage can be remade!"

The next morning, I read those verses and inserted my name, just as our pastor had recommended. That message gave me hope as I prayed, "Dear Lord, I am willing for You to continue working, and I claim these verses as my own."

The days and hours dragged on while the kids and I waited and prayed for Bill's return. I said nothing derogatory about Bill and tried to keep a positive atmosphere in our home. The Holy Spirit prompted me to pray specifically that God would remind Bill of the children and that perhaps even music would speak to his heart.

Finally, after ten days, the Lord spoke to my inner being with the distinct impression that Bill would be coming home and I should prepare for his return. So I quickly began cleaning the house and getting everything in order.

Sure enough, our pastor called that evening. "Amy, I have Bill with me, and he is not feeling well. May I bring him home?"

"Yes!" I exclaimed with excitement and relief. God had answered our prayers! I shared the good news with the children, and when the pastor's car pulled into the driveway, they bolted out the door to tearfully greet their dad. Bill had become physically ill because of the Spirit's conviction over what he had done. He had actually called our pastor to come and get him. Visibly crushed and repentant, Bill later told me how he could not stop thinking about his family and also how a couple of songs just kept coming to mind.

While Bill's affair with Martha had apparently ended, the serious work on our marriage relationship had just begun. At first, things were wonderful. I didn't ask questions because the details were not important to me now that Bill was home with a new sense of commitment.

After a couple of weeks, in accordance with church discipline, Bill and Martha solemnly confessed their sin to the church and asked forgiveness. Many church members had been praying, and it helped us all to get the matter openly resolved. The outpouring of unconditional love to both parties paved the way for healing and restoration. However, with the blessing of our pastor, we temporarily changed churches to avoid awkward situations. Our new church family ministered to us and helped us grow spiritually, but still our marriage remained unstable.

As life got back to "normal," some issues arose that we needed to address. We were not communicating well. I had a tendency to take charge, while Bill's response was to avoid conflict. Many of our problems needed more attention than our pastor could give, so we sought professional Christian counseling. However, our relationship seemed to deteriorate in the midst of it. Bill even threatened to leave again, but I think God used Bill's commitment to our children to keep him at home.

One day in late winter our three kids asked to speak privately with their dad. They took him to the bedroom and closed the door; I later learned that each spoke the truth in love. They basically said, "Dad, you are doing everything you taught us *not* to do." I'm sure that had a huge impact on Bill.

Bill had retrained for a different job and began working for another company. In the meantime, I had lost weight and became so emotionally and physically drained I could hardly move at times. Heightened anxiety resulted in my talking too much, giving Bill suggestions he didn't really need.

One day a wise woman whom I greatly admired counseled me. "Amy," she said thoughtfully, "you cannot be the Holy Spirit. It is His job to convict Bill, not yours. Why don't you try being quiet for a couple of weeks and see what happens? No teaching. No opinions. Just place Bill in God's hands."

Normally, I would have laughed and said, "Me? Quiet for two weeks? No way!" But by this time, I felt like that Jeremiah lump of clay in God the potter's hands. In my weakness, I turned to Him for strength and prayed, *Lord, please help me be quiet for two weeks.* God truly worked during this time as I learned to consciously wait upon Him. He was moving, although I could not see it. I concentrated on holding my tongue, and during my quietness Bill could hear God speak.

At the end of that period, a miracle unfolded. One evening as I passed Bill's chair, he said, "Amy, you are trying so hard." His voice broke and revealed a spirit of humility that I had not seen before. Tears streamed down his cheeks as he arose from his chair and took my hand. When we embraced I knew that we had finally reached a turning point, a genuine breakthrough in our relationship, a defining moment. Healing had begun.

Soon after, we attended a Marriage Encounter weekend during which we discovered that sometimes we could write our feelings to each other rather than speak them. Bill confessed he had allowed his personal relationship with the Lord to deteriorate, and he had used complaints against me to rationalize his behavior. I asked Bill's forgiveness for being preoccupied with other things and not meeting his needs. That weekend, after we verbally renewed our vows to each other, we began to see God's truth revealed in our lives. He promises to redeem past failures, just as He told Judah: "Then I will make up to you for the years that the swarming locust has eaten, the creeping locust, the stripping locust and the gnawing locust, my great army which I sent among you. You will have plenty to eat and be satisfied and praise the name of the LORD your God, who has dealt wondrously with you; then My people will never be put to shame" (Joel 2:25-26).

We are now seeing that promise fulfilled. Not only has God used that difficult time to help us grow in our personal lives, we also have seen the fruit of our commitment in the lives of our grown children. They have each made a choice to honor God and to obey Him in their own marriage relationships. In addition, our ten grandchildren are a great blessing! And to think . . . we could have easily missed all this joy!

Before our marital problems first surfaced, God had prompted me to pray to enlarge my sphere of influence, to better understand *agape* love, and to develop a quiet and gentle spirit. He also knew before Bill left what I would be facing. Since He has answered those requests so clearly, I experienced growth and maturity instead of devastation.

It would have been so easy to give up at many points along the way, but today Bill and I are happier than we have ever been. The "locusts" thought they had a chance to destroy us, but through Him, we told them good-bye. And now we are rejoicing as we celebrate our forty-second wedding anniversary!

Faithlifter
Commitment

IN HER SHOES

As a result of Amy and Bill's working through their problems, the Lord has enlarged Amy's sphere of influence so that many women feel comfortable in seeking her counsel. Because she humbled herself before God, He has given her greater insights, as well as the ability to communicate heart-to-heart with others in distress.

She had prayed to understand *agape* love and discovered that it is unconditional love given without expecting anything in return. After Bill's return, Martha and Amy met together in their pastor's study. Amy knelt at Martha's feet and presented her with a long-stemmed red rose and said, "Martha, I forgive you, and I hold no animosity toward you. I am praying for your marriage, too." Only agape love could have put those words in Amy's mouth and placed true forgiveness in her heart.

She learned that the "gentle and quiet spirit" described in 1 Peter 3:4 did not mean that she had to change her bubbly, outgoing personality, but rather that she could find calmness through confident trust in God.

Has Amy's story revealed sins or weaknesses that you might need to work on? Think about the power of forgiveness. What benefits resulted from this couple's commitment?

IN HIS WORD

Commitment means the binding together by a promise, covenant, pledge, or vow. The Hebrew word for *covenant* means "to cut or divide" and alluded to an ancient sacrificial custom in connection with covenant-making, as when God made a covenant with Abram in Genesis 15:10. The sacrifices were divided.

In contrast, the English word *covenant* means "a coming together, a mutual undertaking between two parties, each binding himself to fulfill obligations." *Covenant* is also the biblical word used to describe the relationship between a husband and wife.

When the Old Testament prophet Malachi became angry at his people for not taking God's Word seriously, he said this: " 'Why has God abandoned us?' you cry. I'll tell you why; it is because the Lord has seen your treachery in divorcing your wives who have been faithful to you through the years, the companions you promised to care for and keep. You were united to your wife by the Lord. In God's wise plan, when you married, the two of you became one person in his sight. And what does he want? Godly children from your union. Therefore, guard your passions! Keep faith with the wife of your youth" (Malachi 2:14-15, TLB).

The men of Malachi's day were divorcing their wives and marrying younger women. They were ignoring the bonding that God had directed in the two becoming one. They also overlooked the spiritual purpose of being united with God. To "guard your passions" meant to have the same commitment to marriage that God has to the promises made to His people. It is important to have passion in a marriage relationship, keeping the intimacy satisfying and the commitment alive. This passion should be always and only for one's spouse, as Malachi taught: "For the Lord, the God of Israel, says he hates divorce and cruel men. Therefore, control your passions—let there be no divorcing of your wives" (Malachi 2:16, TLB).

God created marriage as a gift to Adam and Eve. In Genesis 2:24 He sets forth the basic aspects of a strong marriage:

- A man leaves his father and mother and publicly promises himself to his wife.
- The man and woman are joined together by taking responsibility for one another's welfare.
- They promise to love their mate above all others and become "one flesh" in sexual union, reserved only for the marriage relationship. God's creation of woman from the bone and flesh of a man is a visual affirmation of the "one flesh" concept in marriage (see Genesis 2:23).

Jesus taught about the destructiveness of divorce. "The law of Moses says, 'If anyone wants to be rid of his wife, he can divorce her merely by giving her a letter of dismissal.' But I say that a man who divorces his wife, except for fornication, causes her to commit adultery if she marries again. And he who marries her commits adultery" (Matthew 5:31-32, TLB).

Divorce is as devastating now as it was in Jesus' day. God meant for marriage to be a lifetime commitment. When people marry they should not think of divorce as an easy "out" if relationship problems surface. Nor should they use divorce to abuse the marriage contract and leave their spouses to lust after someone else.

If a spouse does commit adultery, divorce does not have to be the first option. Forgiveness, reconciliation, and restoration should be the goal instead of finding excuses for abandoning the marriage covenant.

IN YOUR LIFE

Let's be honest. Making a marriage relationship work is not easy. Two people from different backgrounds with different temperaments and responses to stress combine to test even the most flexible among us. Add to that all the baggage from past experiences, plus the long list of unspoken spousal expectations, and to "become one flesh" is even a greater challenge. But building a satisfying marriage is one of the greatest joys of life.

All of the above underline the importance of personal commitment. Pastor and author Chip Ingram states, "Personal commitments bring awesome power. They are very powerful. Not just in the spiritual realm. Genuine commitment focuses and increases our attention on the challenge before us. Commitment inspires. Making a personal commitment means we sign up in advance and say, 'I pledge by the grace of God to do this.' Then, when we have a weak moment, we go back to that commitment and say, 'I've already made a decision. I knew when I made that decision that there would be days like this. I made the decision anyway.

I'm not changing my mind based on how I feel this moment."[1]

In their book *Love Extravagantly: Making the Modern Marriage Work*, Marita Littauer and Chuck Noon address the issue of commitment. Many families are comprised of second marriages and stepchildren, in which case many emotional needs surface. Discipline issues, especially involving teens, can really test a marriage. The book describes how one couple, Gene and Lynn, made a pact based on Mark 10:9: "What God has joined together, let no man separate," Gene says. "That included the children." The chapter closes with the admonition, "We encourage you to stand on that Scripture as well—to love each other extravagantly; not to get, but to give, even if you feel like giving up!"[2]

We enter marriage with certain dreams, and before long reality sets in. This observation from the book *Passages of Marriage* rings true: "You don't marry a dream or a way of life; you marry a person. The dream might change, the way of life probably will, and the person certainly will. And so will you. We all do. Your commitment is to that person all the while you're both changing."[3]

The rocky marriage will likely fail under duress if divorce is considered as a possible solution. Perhaps a better approach would be for the husband and wife to renew their commitment before God and maybe even write out their plans.

The coauthors suggest something similar in *Passages of Marriage*:

1. Statement of affirmation; at least one attribute each person admires and appreciates in the other
2. Statement of extent of commitment to the marriage
3. Promise of fidelity
4. Statement of faith
5. Statement of recognition of old, dysfunctional hidden agendas
6. Declaration of new agendas to redress dysfunctions
7. Steps to improve sexual relations
8. Update and revise goals
9. Share specific requests (romantic nights out, companionship)[4]

God's Word teaches us that it is better not to vow than to make a vow and not fulfill it (see Ecclesiastes 5:5). Positive and healthy commitment by both marriage partners is the key to leaving a lasting legacy that will strengthen families for future generations.

CHAPTER SEVENTEEN

My Manager Showed the Way

Sheila Carlson

Teresa fascinated me. She and I worked in a shoe department together, and when a customer came in and tried on ten pairs of shoes without buying any, Teresa remained pleasant and calm. She good-naturedly answered the customer's endless questions while I seethed. "Hey, lady," I wanted to yell, "why don't you just buy a pair of shoes and leave!" *How could Teresa control her temper?*

Because I grew up in a home where we often screamed to get our point across, Teresa's consistent kindness touched me every day. Her short brown hair and winning smile enhanced her wholesome, all-American appearance, but above all, I liked her peaceful countenance. *What makes Teresa different from anyone I've ever known?* I wondered.

As manager of the sporting goods store, twenty-three-year-old Teresa knew what this eighteen-year-old employee needed. One night when only a few customers came in, I wasted time talking with a coworker. Teresa walked to the back of the store. Later I learned she disappeared behind the curtains to pray for wisdom in correcting me. Instead of being critical, Teresa gently guided me with positive words.

"Sheila," she said, "it's always best if you find something to do. That makes my job easier." Her interest sparked my initiative, and I saw chores waiting. I promptly got busy because I wanted to please her and do my best.

When I needed direction, Teresa helped me by first explaining what I was doing well. Then she gave her advice, saying, "It works best for me if I do it this way." She often injected a sense of humor into her instructions that inspired me to try her ideas. I thought, *If it works for her, perhaps it will work for me, too.* I had difficulty dealing with conflict and didn't know how to take constructive criticism, but Teresa's consistent encouragement helped me gain confidence. She also had a talent for helping me think, analyze, and even answer my own questions. In short, Teresa was the kind of role model I needed. I wanted to be like her.

Because I frequently felt a lack of emotional support from my parents, who sometimes left me and my siblings to fend for ourselves, Teresa's sensitivity, concern, and uplifting approach conveyed an unconditional love I had never known. One evening, after I'd worked with her about a month, we talked privately.

"Teresa," I asked, "how do you handle yourself so well? You always seem to know just what to say. I've never met anyone like you."

Teresa revealed it was her faith in Jesus Christ that gave her patience and self-control. She talked about the Bible, how much she enjoyed reading it and applying what it said to everyday living. She even showed me the verses in Matthew about loving your enemies and praying for them. That was foreign to me. *Who was Jesus Christ?* I wondered; the only time I'd heard the name was in cursing.

One day when we had some extra time at the store, Teresa said, "Sheila, tell me more about yourself."

I explained that I was born in Germany of a German mother and an American GI father, both of whom I never knew. My real mother could not take care of me, so when I was eleven months old, she put an ad in the church bulletin to find me a home. My adoptive parents, a U.S. military family stationed in Germany, learned about it and brought me back to the U.S. to live. I do not harbor any bitterness against them now because they did the best they could, but they did not set a good example.

Tobacco and alcohol abuses were problems. I felt emotionally abandoned and, as a result, made many wrong choices. Basically I was angry and rebellious. Now, as a new bride in a new town with no friends, I had no sense of direction for my life. I didn't even know how to cook. My husband, a law enforcement officer, was a kind and compassionate man, but he had his difficulties, too. In short, I was struggling.

Then I turned to Teresa and asked, "How about yourself?"

She had been married about five years. Her husband was a believer when they married, but she was from a home similar to mine. She had received Christ shortly after her marriage. She said, "Sheila, when I tried to share my faith with my dad, he became furious."

Teresa and I had worked together for almost a year when she invited me to her home. She was a wonderful friend because she cared about my spiritual condition. That evening as I was leaving, our conversation turned to the "end times." Teresa explained what the Bible said in Revelation about the world's destruction and that she would not be there because she would be with Jesus. Then she asked, "Do you want to come with me?"

I knew I didn't want to be left behind. So on that evening in 1988 in Teresa's driveway, I bowed my head, prayed the sinner's prayer, and felt a tremendous burden lifted. Afterward, Teresa hugged me and rejoiced but warned that hard times would eventually test my faith.

In the ensuing days, my husband, Steve, noticed a change in me, but he did not respond positively at first. He later told me, "I wondered what Teresa had done to you." He was not interested in the Bible or in hearing about Christ. So Teresa advised me to just quietly pray for him and continue attending church. I did.

Sadly, Teresa and her husband moved away, but the Lord, in His wisdom, sent a mature Christian neighbor who taught me how to memorize Scripture. While I concentrated on spiritual growth, my Sunday school class joined me in praying for Steve. They never gave up; they believed the Lord would touch his life, too. It was no coincidence that a new coworker befriended my husband and witnessed to him during that time.

One year later, Steve voluntarily attended church, and I felt thrilled when he stepped forward to openly confess his faith. He later told me he had received Christ one day while alone in our home, but after hearing the pastor's sermon that morning, he felt he should not keep it a secret. His step of faith opened a new chapter in our lives.

Through the years, we have been growing together. As parents of two sons and a daughter, we are concentrating on maintaining a Christ-centered home. Steve is leading our family and constantly seeking God's will in our marriage, in parenting, and in his profession. I have asked my parents' forgiveness for my bad attitude, and our relationship has been restored.

Both sides of our extended families have observed us and wondered, *What happened?* I joyfully report that, with the passing of time, both my brother and sister have received Christ. By God's grace, Steve and I are letting our lights shine . . . all because my manager showed the way.

Faithlifter
Belief

IN HER SHOES

With whom do you identify most in the story—Teresa or Sheila? What characteristics set Teresa apart as she encountered difficult situations at the store?

After writing this story, I realized once again how our behavior mirrors our beliefs. If a discrepancy exists between the words we speak and the actions we take, an observer will place the actions before the words. Teresa's words matched her actions. That is why she was able to deliver a message of hope from God's Word that Sheila could readily receive.

Sheila's difficult background caused her to take note of Teresa's approach to life. God used the contrasting lifestyles to inject hunger for Him in Sheila's heart. Perhaps without knowing it, you are demonstrating godly characteristics to someone who is watching. Or maybe you are the one who wonders, *How can I find peace, order, and hope in my life?*

IN HIS WORD

Belief is the first step in coming to faith in Christ. One New Testament Greek word for *belief* indicates action. Jesus first used the verb when He asked Nathaniel, "Do you believe?" (John 1:50).

Conversion is one of the most joyful events known to man. Even the angels in heaven rejoice when a sinner is saved! Another word for *conversion* is *salvation*, the starting point for the Holy Spirit's work within a person to begin changing his entire being. Our salvation from hell—eternal separation from God—starts with the basic belief that Jesus is God Incarnate, God in the flesh, just as the Bible says.

The deity of Christ is expressed in the book of John: "I and the Father are one" (John 10: 30).

When should we believe?

"The time is fulfilled, and the kingdom of God is at hand; repent and believe in the gospel" (Mark 1:15).

What happens when we believe?

"Believe in the Lord Jesus, and you will be saved, you and your household" (Acts 16:31).

"Truly, truly, I say to you, he who believes has eternal life" (John 6:47).

How can we know if we have believed?

"This is His commandment, that we believe in the name of His Son Jesus Christ, and love one another, just as He commanded us. The one who keeps His commandments abides in Him, and He in him. We know by this that He abides in us, by the Spirit whom He has given us" (1 John 3:23-24).

Do we sometimes struggle even if we know what is right?

"Immediately the boy's father cried out and said, 'I do believe; help my unbelief'" (Mark 9:24). Often we can identify with the father of the demon-possessed son. We want to believe but find it difficult. The disciples in this case were unable to help the man's son. They lost power because apparently they were trusting in their own abilities. Jesus recommended prayer: "This kind cannot come out by anything but prayer" (verse 29). Jesus said, "All things are possible to him who believes" (verse 23).

God always knows what is best, even when we don't understand all the mysteries of belief and faith and how they fit together.

IN YOUR LIFE

In 1 Peter 3:15 we are admonished to be ready to tell others about our faith in Christ: "But sanctify Christ as Lord in your hearts, always being ready to make a defense to everyone who asks you to give an account for the hope that is in you, yet with gentleness and reverence."

Many women in the workplace, like Sheila, are searching for meaning in life, healing of past hurts, and eternal security. Here are a few ideas that might help in sharing your faith with the unsaved:

Be ready.
Think about your personal testimony and write it out in different lengths—perhaps one-minute, five-minute, and ten-minute versions. Consider the main points, especially what you believe was "the turning point." Practice speaking your testimony into a tape recorder and then listen to it. Think about how you would feel if you did not know Christ and heard your testimony. Does it sound preachy? Judgmental? Is the tone open and loving? Is the terminology understandable? Is it appealing? Prepare and then pray for an opportunity to share. Let the Holy Spirit lead you.

Be sensitive and sympathetic.
We all have pressures and family problems from time to time. When someone needs a sympathetic ear, be willing to listen. Sometimes a death in the family can become an opportunity to bring up spiritual things and share a brief testimony. You might begin the conversation, "Has anyone ever shared how you can *know* you're going to heaven when you die? I wouldn't want to go without you." Showing interest in another person's soul is a powerful tool.

Share a book with a Christian theme.
Whether it's a practical handbook on parenting or marriage or coping with life's hardships, a novel, a biography, or a collection of inspirational stories, any number of books from a Christian perspective can be a witness to a seeker. An easy-to-understand Bible paraphrase such as *The Living Bible* or *The Message* can be a timely gift of love to someone who needs Jesus.

Move from small talk to substance.

Sometimes talking about the headlines or a new movie can open the door to planting seeds of grace. There's no need to pretend you "have it all together." A little transparency about a fault or failure may lead to your confession that none of us can live this life in our own strength.

Offer to pray.

If someone has a need or you sense she's having a "down day," just ask, "Is there something I could pray about for you?" Almost everyone appreciates such an offer, and very few will reject it. Let the Holy Spirit guide you in knowing whether you should pray right then or if you should pray privately, on your own.

Tap into mutual on-line support.

Did you know that more than half of Internet users are now women and girls? By just typing in "Christian Women's Groups" in your search engine, you can find help and also a place to give encouragement. You can grow in Christ, mentor a new believer, or gain ideas from other women on a variety of topics. Here are some on-line sites to check out:

The Proverbs 31 Ministry (www.gospelcom.net/p31/) discusses concerns about marriage and raising children and provides encouragement for building godly homes. An Internet magazine designed to encourage women in their daily walk, www.christianwomentoday.com, includes articles on discipleship and tips on witnessing.[1]

I prayed for faith and thought it would strike me like lightning. But faith did not come. One day I read, 'Now faith comes by hearing, and hearing by the Word of God.' I had closed my Bible and prayed for faith. I now began to study my Bible and faith has been growing ever since.

—Dwight L. Moody

Notes

Introduction
1. Nancy Sanders, "A Singer Who Shares," *The Christian Communicator* 5, no. 10 (October 1993), p. 2.
2. Eleanor Doan, *The New Speaker's Sourcebook* (Grand Rapids, Mich.: Zondervan Publishing House, 1968), p. 151.

Chapter 1
1. H. Norman Wright, "When Mom Is a Perfectionist," *Focus on the Family* (August 1991), pp. 2-3.
2. J. Dwight Pentecost, *The Joy of Fellowship: A Study of First John* (Grand Rapids, Mich.: Lamplighter Books, Zondervan Publishing House, 1977), p. 87.
3. Jose Luis Gonzalez-Balado, *Mother Teresa, In My Own Words* (New York: Gramercy Books, 1996), p. 34.

Chapter 2
1. Oswald Chambers, *Faith: A Holy Walk* (Grand Rapids, Mich.: Discovery House Publishers, 1999), p. 87.

Chapter 3
1. Jerry Bridges, *Trusting God: Even When Life Hurts* (Colorado Springs, Colo.: NavPress, 1988), p. 143.
2. Bridges, p. 18.

Chapter 4
1. Charles H. Spurgeon, *Faith's Checkbook* (Chicago: Moody Press, 1987), p. 63.

Chapter 5
1. John White, *Parents in Pain* (Downers Grove, Ill.: InterVarsity Press, 1979), p. 44.

2. John Blanchard, *Gathered Gold: A Treasury of Quotations for Christians* (Hertfordshire, England: Evangelical Press, 1984), p. 108.

3. Mart DeHaan, "Been Thinking About Forgiveness," *Times of Discovery* 60, no. 1 (January 1999), p. 1. Used with permission.

4. DeHaan, p. 1.

5. Blanchard, p. 108.

6. Don Anderson, *Drawing Closer, Growing Stronger: Making the Most of Your Walk with God* (Sisters, Oreg.: Multnomah, 1997), p. 159. Used by permission of Don Anderson. All rights reserved. (Available through www.DonAndersonMinistries.org.)

7. DeHaan, p. 1.

8. Lewis B. Smedes, *Forgive and Forget: Healing the Hurts We Don't Deserve* (New York: Pocket Books, 1984), p. 131.

Chapter 6

1. Ken Gire, *The Reflective Life* (Colorado Springs, Colo.: Chariot Victor Publishing, 1998), p. 7.

Chapter 7

1. Marvin Olasky, ed., "Let's Roll," *World* 17, no. 31 (August 17, 2002), pp. 24-25.

2. John Blanchard, *Gathered Gold: A Treasury of Quotations for Christians* (Hertfordshire, England: Evangelical Press, 1984), p. 153.

Chapter 8

1. Beth Moore, *Breaking Free: Making Liberty in Christ a Reality in Life* (Nashville: LifeWay Press, 1999), pp. 115-136.

2. Cynthia Spell Humbert, *Deceived by Shame, Desired by God* (Colorado Springs, Colo.: NavPress, 2001), p. 133.

3. Jim Cymbala, *The Life God Blesses: The Secret of Enjoying God's Favor* (Grand Rapids, Mich.: Zondervan, 2001), p. 60.

4. Philip Yancey, *What's So Amazing About Grace?* (Grand Rapids, Mich.: Zondervan Publishing House, 1997), p. 272.

5. Yancey, front flap of book jacket.
6. Julia H. Johnston and Daniel B. Towner, "Grace Greater Than Our Sin," *Hymns Tried and True* (Chicago, Ill.: The Bible Institute Colportage Association, 1911).

Chapter 9
1. J. Sidlow Baxter, *Does God Still Guide?* (Grand Rapids, Mich.: Zondervan Publishing House, 1968), pp. 140-141.
2. Elisabeth Elliot, *Elisabeth Elliot Newsletter* (July/August 1995), p. 1.
3. John Blanchard, *Gathered Gold: A Treasury of Quotations for Christians* (Hertfordshire, England: Evangelical Press, 1984), p. 210.
4. Blanchard, p. 209.

Chapter 10
1. James C. Dobson, *When God Doesn't Make Sense* (Wheaton, Ill.: Tyndale House Publishers, 1993), pp. 17-18.
2. Jerry Bridges, *Trusting God: Even When Life Hurts* (Colorado Springs, Colo.: NavPress, 1988), p. 52.

Chapter 11
1. Sheila Walsh, *Living Fearlessly* (Grand Rapids, Mich.: Zondervan Publishing House, 2001), p. 26.
2. Paul E. Billheimer, *Destined for the Cross* (Wheaton, Ill.: Tyndale House Publishers, 1987), p. 62.
3. Harry Verploegh, *The Oswald Chambers Devotional Reader* (Nashville: Thomas Nelson Publishers, 1990), p. 81.
4. Hannah Whitall Smith, *The Christian's Secret of a Happy Life* (Westwood, N.J.: Barbour Books, 1985), p. 44.
5. Jerry Bridges, *Trusting God: Even When Life Hurts* (Colorado Springs, Colo.: NavPress, 1988), p. 142.

Chapter 12
1. Paul Thigpen, "Our Joyful God," *Discipleship Journal*, no. 124 (July/August 2001), pp. 37-39.

2. Charles Swindoll, *Laugh Again* (Dallas: Word Publishing, 1992), p. 34.
3. Oswald Chambers, *Faith: A Holy Walk* (Grand Rapids, Mich.: Discovery House Publishers, 1999), p. 98.

Chapter 13

1. Oswald Chambers, *My Utmost for His Highest* (New York: Dodd, Mead, 1963), p. 79.
2. Jerry Bridges, *Trusting God: Even When Life Hurts* (Colorado Springs, Colo.: NavPress, 1988), pp. 127-128.

Chapter 14

1. Warren Wiersbe, *God Isn't in a Hurry: Learning to Slow Down and Live* (Grand Rapids, Mich.: Baker Books, 1994), pp. 54-55.
2. Tom Carter, compiler, *2,200 Quotations from the Writings of Charles Haddon Spurgeon* (Grand Rapids, Mich.: Baker Books, 1988), p. 357.

Chapter 15

1. J. Vernon McGee, *Death of a Little Child* (Pasadena, Calif.: Thru the Bible Radio, 1970), p. 17.
2. Joyce Landorf, *Mourning Song* (Old Tappan, N.J.: Fleming H. Revell Company, 1974), p. 167.
3. Fran Caffey Sandin, *See You Later, Jeffrey* (Wheaton, Ill.: Tyndale House Publishers, 1988). Contact author for permissions or purchase.

Chapter 16

1. Chip Ingram, *Holy Ambition: What It Takes to Make a Difference for God* (Chicago: Moody Press, 2002), pp. 151-152, 155.
2. Marita Littauer and Chuck Noon, *Love Extravagantly: Making the Modern Marriage Work* (Minneapolis: Bethany House, 2001), p. 128.

3. Frank Minirth et al., *Passages of Marriage: Five Growth Stages That Will Take Your Marriage to Greater Intimacy and Fulfillment* (Nashville: Thomas Nelson Publishers, 1991), p. 62.

4. Minirth et al., p. 105.

Chapter 17

1. Tricia Goyer, "Making Connections," *Home Life* 56, no. 11 (August 2002), p. 41.

For Further Reading

Henry, Matthew. *Matthew Henry's Commentary in One Volume.* Grand Rapids: Zondervan Publishing House, 1961.

Smith, William. *Smith's Bible Dictionary,* Revised Edition. Nashville: Holman Bible Publishers, 1986.

Strong, James. *The New Strong's Exhaustive Concordance of the Bible.* Nashville: Thomas Nelson Publishers, 1990.

Vine, W. E. *An Expository Dictionary of New Testament Words.* Old Tappan, N.J.: Fleming H. Revell Company, 1966.

About the Author

FRAN CAFFEY SANDIN is a registered nurse and a popular guest speaker for various women's events in the United States and Canada. An organist in her church, Fran also is active in women's ministries and co-teaches a couples' class with her physician-husband, James. One of five Greenville, Texas, writers who call themselves "Hens with Pens," she coauthored the bestseller *Courage for the Chicken-Hearted* and its sequel, *Eggstra Courage for the Chicken-Hearted* (both Honor Books). Fran, a graduate of Texas Woman's University, has authored many magazine articles, has contributed to ten other books, and wrote *See You Later, Jeffrey* (Tyndale House). She and James enjoy sailing, snow skiing, traveling, hiking, and walking Honey, their yellow Labrador retriever. The Sandins have a young adult son, a married daughter, and two granddaughters.

Active over the years in Bible Study Fellowship, Fran wants to encourage women by introducing them to Jesus and helping them to grow in faith through the practical application of Scripture in daily living. If you or someone you know has been touched by this book, she would enjoy hearing from you at sandin@pulse.net, or you can visit her web site at www.fransandin.com.